Landscapes of Wilderness

Other Books by the Author

Bastar Dispatches: A Passage Through the Wilds
A Sense of Home—Abujhmad and a Childhood Village

Landscapes of Wilderness

Narendra

HarperCollins *Publishers* India

First published in India by HarperCollins *Publishers* 2024
4th Floor, Tower A, Building No. 10, DLF Cyber City,
DLF Phase II, Gurugram, Haryana – 122002
www.harpercollins.co.in

2 4 6 8 10 9 7 5 3 1

Copyright © Narendra 2024

P-ISBN: 978-93-5699-533-8
E-ISBN: 978-93-5699-534-5

The views and opinions expressed in this book are the author's own and the facts are as reported by him, and the publishers are not in any way liable for the same.

Narendra asserts the moral right
to be identified as the author of this work.

All rights reserved. No part of this publication may be reproduced, stored in a retrieval system, or transmitted, in any form or by any means, electronic, mechanical, photocopying, recording or otherwise, without the prior permission of the publishers.

Typeset in 11.5/15 Sabon LT Std at
Manipal Technologies Limited, Manipal

Printed and bound at
Nutech Print Services - India

This book is printed on FSC® certified paper
which ensures responsible forest management.

To the average and common people living ordinary, non-descript lives in India's countryside

Contents

	Foreword	ix
	Introduction	xiii
1.	'Silence Is Also Conversation'	1
2.	State and the Simpleton	7
3.	Outside the Doorframe	16
4.	Barber's Tales	19
5.	Ten Feet of the World	29
6.	There Showed a Tree	32
7.	Gender Relations in the Wilds	35
8.	Burunga the Blacksmith	45
9.	I Sat By	49
10.	They Were Seiks	52
11.	Conversations on the Way	58
12.	Tiger in the Twilight	68
13.	Of Parvati's Wedding	74
14.	Chandan bhai	79
15.	Strangers, Friends and Well-Wishers—My Good Samaritans	83

Contents

16.	Tellings of the Fields	93
17.	Sarup the Neanderthal	97
18.	Cacophonies	101
19.	Official Woes—Of Housing, Toilets and Bullocks	105
20.	Four Feet of Dadạngir	109
21.	Without a Story or Stride	112
22.	Mumblings and Miscellanies	116
23.	Bear Atop the Roof	128
24.	'What Are You Nothing About'	133
25.	Traditional Bastar—Amongst Healers	137
26.	Trail and the Writer's Chore	144
27.	Writing as Municipal—Word, Landscape and People	148
28.	Tin, Tarpaulin and Bamboo Poles	151
29.	Atop the Graveyard Wall	155
30.	All Said and Done	159
31.	Vultures in the Sky	163
32.	Inner Journeys, External Mappings	167
33.	Thieving the Beggar	175
34.	The Illiterate World	180
35.	Un-Noticing and Unheeding	184
36.	Many Walked That Day	188
37.	Makar Sankranti	193
38.	Of Identity, Eluding and the Place	201
39.	On a Birthday	210
	Acknowledgements	219

Foreword

WILDERNESS, villages and countrysides have had a deep pull for me. Their people have had a special appeal. Fortunately, a significant part of my life has been spent in such environs. A part of my early childhood in the late 1950s and the early '60s was spent in my native village in north India.

Though many still survive in different parts of the country, wilderness villages and landscapes are rapidly shrinking today. But those that have lived for thousands of years do not erase overnight. For the people, land and landscape were like religion. Theirs were not organized or efficient communities, nor were such considered desirable. Organized religions and other 'isms' did come but could not fully root themselves here. Till even fifty or sixty years ago, the wilderness and the village lived—and still do to some extent—quite outside the issues and parameters of 'isms' and all they entail. People lived on land.

It has its mystique. It joined humans in a delicate coherence to the skies, vast vacant spaces, waters, the vegetation, animals and the little gods and goddesses that, too, lived on it. Human society was incomplete without them. When I was a child in my village, people did not much know of gods in the skies, worship, temples, beliefs and elaborate rituals. The significance, or otherwise, of being human stood different. Fortunately, ordinary human society was still not so tied to the singularities of enlightenment, change or progress.

Alas, the survival of the wild and village now depends on the very destruction of their landscape. The majority of our villages now live with depleted lands, skies, waters, *veerans* (vast and vacant spaces), animals, birds, gods, goddesses, ancestors and their associated richness. That way of life where the hum of stillness was distinctly discernible to the accustomed ear is almost gone. That way of life fostered generous sensitivities, conviviality, cohesions and continuities. Living outside contemporary issues and parameters, life was grounded and native as against the pan-Indian or global. Sustained interaction between humans and landscape brought a certain ethos, modes of living, governance and non-profit economies. Coexistence and mutuality derived organically from living on land as an obvious corollary, instead of the political and studied necessities for survival now. Deep truths were revealed in simple ways of everyday concerns, conversations and conduct. Instead, now there is a singular global grid of politico-economic and knowledge systems to which people's destinies are tied in seemingly irreversible servitude.

When I first reached Bastar and its Abujhmad in 1980, I found that these areas did not have even villages; more so Abujhmad. Abujhmad could be described as pre-society. In the region's core area of 1,500 square kilometres, the three or four bamboo-and-thatch huts (almost indistinguishable from the surrounding dense vegetation) that lay about did not fit the criteria of forming villages as we understand them. They were without hierarchies and preoccupations such as farming, carpentry, pottery, blacksmith, weaving or any form of trade. At best and worst, they could be described as dispersed settlements. Contemporary lexicons may not have a word for them. My earlier two books, *Bastar Dispatches: Passage through the Wilds* and *A Sense of Home: From Abujhmad to Childhood Village* (HarperCollins India, 2018 and 2020 respectively), dwell on more as such.

The pages that follow predominantly have wilderness and landscape as the major referents. I have attempted to provide some glimpses of the richness of India's countryside, and of the raw wisdom that comes straight from the soil and the heart. The two were indivisible. In these pages the reader will meet some individuals who lived by an un-hewn and simple ethos, seemingly bovine in their ways and demeanour. Theirs was good and honest living—one that did not need God or Constitution to be simple and civil.

Introduction

IN my previous two books—*Bastar Dispatches: Passage through the Wilds* and *A Sense of Home: From Abujhmad to Childhood Village*—I have written of my experiences and observations in the wilds, *adivasis* (tribal people) and folk communities. This book is about the wilds, lands and landscapes, and their intrinsic relationship with the dwellers. Landscapes create worldviews, dispositions, vocabularies and the cadence of everyday living; as though people grow straight out of the earth. There is also an 'inarticulable' element to such relationships. Landscape has its *svabhav* (inner disposition or temperament) and people resonate in coherence and mutuality with it. There is the alikeness of rhythms, flows and paces. In one way or the other, people's gait, postures, facial expressions, speech and silence are of the same timbre as of the hills, streams, vegetation, vacant and abandoned spaces, shadows, stillness and animals—a confluence of human and the rest.

Experiences and ruminations as these occurred when I lived amidst such communities for a certain duration of time. They would not have occurred the way they did had it not been for these regions of sparse countries. This book is a humble attempt at telling that unchanging dormancy and stillness inherent in life's activity and locomotion. I have tried to tell of the trails, trees, waters, veerans, architectures, animals, anthills, skies, ancestors, houses and their people who together constituted the landscape. Neither could have been without the other. Adivasis or not, no matter which part of India (or maybe the world), people and landscapes reside in close intimacy, their bearings and dispositions are common and shared. In some measure, the book also seeks to dwell on the humdrum and commonplace in everyday living—its richness and banality, where gods and divinity are both worshipped and scorned.

Many parts of the book are in the first person and somewhat anecdotal. It is so mainly because the 'anecdotal' or story-like is the very way in our countryside. As against the national or global, anecdote is local or regional. It does not transgress them. That gives it authenticity and legs to stand on. Its vitality dies when it goes beyond the locality. Without an anecdote or two, a conversation in the countryside is not complete or satisfying. Also, the experiences and ruminations I write of happened to me; what better can I speak of than them?

In one way or the other, my first two books could be described as being of topicality and contemporaneity. Though grounded in people and situations, this book is bereft of such express significance and relevance. It is open-ended and loose in narrative. That is how the wilds, villages and lands are. It is neither my intention nor do I have the ability to write a formal sociological work. Sociological writing has its guiding parameters and arguments. In such a work, much may have to be said differently; there is much indiscernible to wilds, villages and landscapes. The chapters herein are more like a traveller's tales. Tales that abide not in the straight and narrow but in the byways and hideaways; tales that have no noticeable worth in contemporary times even though such un-noticeability could be their lasting strength. Almost always, a tale has something that is ever shrouded, obscure and asleep. In sleep it gathers itself. Of not much substance or weight it may be, but I hope the book holds some interest for the reader.

Till even fifty or sixty years ago the above spirit and ethos lived in our wilds, villages and landscapes. Much lived in those lands. Many levels and ways of living and dying came to and from there. Though communities lived in regions separated by hundreds of kilometres, they shared the mystique of land and landscape. Be it Chandan bhai, Sarup, the elder Musahar, Ram Singh's wife or the village of Dedhuki in Saurashtra that staged the Mahabharat on Dussehra (Hindu day of triumph of good over evil when Ram slew Ravan), the people of inscrutable Abujhmad or the elders of my childhood village (who held opposites as true and relevant in the same breath) lived in quite the same way. Living far, far away from each other and speaking different dialects, they had neither met nor heard of each other.

With a vocabulary of no more than 300–500 words, counting up to five, and a sensibility that comes from the primitive wilds, it was in Abujhmad that my musings and mumblings as such began in a somewhat noticeable way. They began hesitantly; the hesitation being still there. Accompanied by the spoken word there was, paradoxically, a persistent silence and stillness to Abujhmad. This was also there in folk landscapes in other parts of the country; an intrinsic silence that unaccustomed ears may not hear. Such is the symbiotic relationship between a word and its muteness that without one the other cannot be. Silence overshadows the substance, and spoken word adds to the stillness. When word has only substance and meaning, it has little. That caused for me the unintelligibility of the regions. Almost involuntarily recalling my childhood village or my travels to other areas in Gujarat, Karnataka, Himachal Pradesh, Tamil Nadu, Bihar, Jharkhand, Maharashtra, Madhya Pradesh, Rajasthan and Uttarakhand amongst others, I found that the different dialects nurtured words and their inseparable silence.

There were no symbols of what is commonly understood as the human civilization in Abujhmad. The Abujhmadia lived outside civilization—in wild Nature. In the folk countryside, there were only a few symbols as such. There were far more of hills, streams, vegetation, vacant and abandoned spaces, shadows, the quiet and animals.

Word, as we understand, does not exist in Nature. On the other hand, word cannot be without civilization. Civilization may be of some social significance but in Nature it means little or nothing. It is incongruent with what exists in landscapes. The very impulse of civilization and its word is to explicate; to convey meaning, substance and significance—which form the very foundations of civilization and its intelligibility. Meaning or substance are a formulation, just as democracy is another. Without intelligibility neither civilization nor its word can be. The modern world and its discourse have been particularly intent on this account. Perhaps this book does not accord well with that project.

How then to write of wordless landscapes, un-intelligibility, intrinsic silences and their people? Or, is it even desirable to write of such? Admittedly, I do not have an answer.

The book is of such background.

Introduction

I must also confess that I have hazarded to write even though there is not the clarity on what I wished to write. Perhaps this absence of clarity, the very nebulousness, is also the book's strength. Sensations, thoughts and situations have travelled to, and away from, each other as though conversing amongst themselves, and occasionally with me. As they came there was to them more of unintelligibility and less of intelligibility. Deep within, persists the feeling that what is being said here is not mine nor I its. It disowns me just as I do it. It is not easy for me to ascertain how much a chapter has said of what wanted to be said. It rarely matches. Each chapter decides its own threshold.

The word 'nebulous' occurs several times in the course of the book. There is a deep nebulousness within and without. At some fortuitous point in life they may come face to face. Such could be moments of deep despair and deep poise; happening as though on their own. Driven as I was by clarity, I could eventually be only a helpless witness to the nebulousness of Abujhmad or landscapes elsewhere; now I am grateful for that helplessness. That 'helplessness' vis-a-vis the magnitude of Abujhmad's densely intertwined and indiscernible wilds persists to this day. Abujhmad or other regions are not something to help oneself with. They only re-present one to oneself and things fall in place; yet nothing does and it remains the same.

It is not the book's intention to critique modernity, its systems, institutions or processes. Its overriding concerns are the wilds, lands, landscapes and their dwellers. Critiquing is not the way of those who dwell in wilderness and landscapes. On the contrary, they dissolve and assimilate. Any critique herein is unintended and inadvertent.

There are thirty-nine chapters in the book. They are gatherings from my wanderings and travels over the years. A large part of these years were, however, spent in Bastar.

Introduction

Photography was prohibited in Abujhmad. Pictures in the book were taken by me in areas geographically contiguous to it. Travels and wanderings, along with the landscapes I found myself in, brought some ruminations and ponderings on my own self, too. In my understanding as their author, the chapters correspond in one way or another to wilderness, obscurity and open-endedness. Like the people or situations they are about, each chapter is different from the other, yet not so. Some chapters are about places such as Ehnar in Abujhmad, some about rivers such as the Kuari in Chambal ravines, some about the *reti* (desolate stretch of sand dunes, spread over a kilometre or two like an immense mythological python) of my childhood village, some about people like Burunga, Chandan bhai or Sarup, and yet others about the lay of the land in some village or the other; some chapters deal with concrete situations, others that may not prominently seem to do so. Yet, in my experience and mind, they are alike in their innate svabhav.

The book is about the inscrutabilities of the mentioned regions and their dwellers. Sometimes language and sentence construction might seem abrupt or incomplete; they have had to be modulated lest the cadence and flow of places and their dwellers go away.

I leave it to you, dear reader, if need be, to connect the dots in the book. Perhaps, many times, it may not be necessary. I cannot say.

Narendra

1
'Silence Is Also Conversation'
—*Ramanna Maharishi*

As I began moving deeper into the interiors of Abujhmad many things occurred that may not have otherwise. Movement happened in stages. It was not planned to move thus. When a phenomenon is unusual one cannot have plans. Abujhmad seemed like a vast ancient silence of centuries; of stillness and its speechlessness. It was also the region for awe and humbleness that comes from being a human there. As time went by came the impression that there was little or nothing to think about or do here. After many months of doing nothing, the reflex to think or do began slowly fading away.

Thought needs an object; as does action. Unless driven thus both wither away. By and by I stopped taking field notes. The study project—the purpose behind my being in Abujhmad—also dropped. It happened on its own. What was there to take notes about or study? Moreover, the region turned out to be outside the purview and reach of research, any research. Gradually, like the Abujhmadias, I too happened to begin only living. There were a few visits to some other 'villages' but they were no more than a handful. In any case, walking those trails was not easy, memorable though they were. The density of dark vegetation and the continuous bends in the trails made the way hazardous; owing to the thickness of vegetation, at times visibility was no more than three or four feet. There were slippery slopes, huge boulders, tall anthills and caves through which ran several dark tunnels for several kilometres across the hills. They all seemed to say something. Also, anything could be lurking around the next bend—from a sleeping wild animal on the ground to a massive beehive on a low-hanging and hidden branch. Above all, one needed a companion to walk with. Mostly, people were unwilling to go anywhere nor did they have a task or reason that required it. There was little or nothing one could do on one's own when the others did little or nothing. Like taking notes or holding conversations, the others considered my visits, too, as needless activities. Any activity beyond the absolutely necessary, it seemed, was considered a hindrance to good living.

It was also a region of solitude. Most times solitude was about the only 'activity' one could indulge in. Who does not like solitude? But I was not prepared for so much of it. There was practically nothing to preoccupy oneself with. Living it day after day and year after year, many times it did seem irksome. One was left with far too much of oneself, alone and nothing. Many times, I needed the comfort of humdrum and everyday human activities like drinking a glass of tea at a shack, a walk through the market, banal conversations, and washing clothes and dishes that make up an average human life. About twice a week the village would go food gathering. There was very little hunting, except of small game like jungle fowl, rats, crabs and fish. People were fond of meat but not inclined to the exertion of hunting. Food gathering involved far less activity. There was much singing, storytelling, joking, leg-pulling and leisure. For days and weeks nothing would happen. Months would go by. About the only event or news would be when a neighbour's goat was lifted by a leopard at night from amidst the sleeping family or when a cobra whooshed into a hut or a cow killed by a tiger failed to return with the herd in the evening. But these happened once in a blue moon. Many times, I wanted to go back to Delhi. But the nearest road lay some seventy kilometres away; in between lay the wilds. There was not available a companion to walk with. I felt as remote and isolated as Abujhmad itself.

I found myself 'killing time'. I would often unwillingly walk to the little Dadangir, 1,000 yards away from my hut; sit by its side and listen to the tiny waves that gurgled but never made another sound. Or I stared at the skies of many blues and empty clouds as ancient as the patch of earth I sat upon. Barring vultures and jungle fowl, never did I spot a bird. Many times, my time was spent in a drowsy wait for the twice-a-week 2.30 p.m. flight from Raipur to Bhubaneshwar—that was my only preoccupation. I could only hear but not see the aeroplane for it flew by at some distance. I could not go for walks. 'A walk in a deep forest' is a misnomer. Walks do not fit into the wild's scheme of things. Only one who does not know this would think of a walk here.

Yet, paradoxically, Abujhmad and its solitude never pressed themselves upon one; that was the region's ease with itself and its dwellers. Abujhmad and its solitude were overwhelming but not imposing. Slowly, as time went by there no longer remained the wish to engage much with the other dwellers of the seven huts in the village. They were themselves disinclined to engage with each other or me. That is what the svabhav of the wilds was. Slowness and vacancy gradually became a habit. Wild Nature grows on one undetected.

In that awe and endearing grandeur lived a quiet. No wonder the Abujhmadias spoke so little. One did not have to learn of the 'quiet', 'stillness' and 'speechlessness' nor to sit down and 'meditate'; Abujhmad itself was meditative. These words were missing from the vocabulary. Interestingly, the quality and texture of a peoples' vocabulary itself is a window into the world they have made for themselves. By this yardstick—the Abujhmadia's yardstick—advanced languages signify meaningless and noisy speech. They communicate, at best, the loss of one's being. Willy-nilly, languages reflect one's quarrels within, with the landscape and with the world. Like the monsters of yore who fed on humans, languages have turned themselves upon their speakers.

Abujhmad lived comfortably, without grouse or discomfort. There was a disinterestedness and passivity, a repose that pre-empted response and engagement even with oneself.

Gradually, the sense of emptiness and futility that comes as a consequence of having no practical output in life began fading away. But nothing came in lieu. The adage 'Nature abhors a vacuum' seemed like a lie. Just as my neighbours, I was left with life, time and passivity. It was an un-interfered and un-varying solitude and non-doing; un-pressed and unseen by any. Solitude is ever the nebulous unseen.

Once or twice a year I would go to Delhi. But I would return after fifteen or twenty days. The inert had its unaccountable pull.

Bhuri *bai*, an illiterate elderly woman in Rajasthan, is revered as a saint. She used to say, 'Silence is the means, silence the end; in silence alone abides silence; only the silent understands silence; one who understands falls silent.' The word '*chup*' (be quiet) stood inscribed at the entrance to her house. Her message to her disciples was, 'Be quiet, say nothing.' Abujhmad had not heard of Bhuri *bai* or her life and legend. Yet, Abujhmad and Bhuri *bai* were the same.

The wilds of Abujhmad filled me with something that I had not known earlier. As with everyone else everywhere, it had already been within but I had not known. It could be only faintly sensed in some ways but even today I may not be able to adequately articulate it even though each line in the book is about it. Abujhmad was where everything came together— and yet nothing did—in a way as if they had never been apart. There may perhaps be some possible overstatements or understatements in my writings on Abujhmad, but probably never a departure from what the region spoke of albeit dimly. It came as a flow and I found myself in a situation where I either had to accept or dismiss it. These choices are probably never made consciously, leave alone rationally; but choices do get made. Somehow, things fall in place with something within that one never clearly knew about.

If we lived in wild and unsullied Nature, the bulk of our Truth, gods, scriptures, learnings, concerns and consciousness would collapse. The heavy baggage of values, visions, ethics and utopia gathered over thousands of years will collapse, too. We have invested so much in God, Truth, State and democracy and the rest that eventually, this way or that, they have become guidelines for human existence where none is needed. They have also become causes to live and even die for. Many make a living out of them. Even the notion of human society—whose indispensability and role I never had doubted earlier—began to appear as the progenitor of needlessness about being human. Wild does not allow for human society; trees, tigers, rivers and hills have not constituted one despite many of them being older on earth than us. Intrinsically, man is not social. Man is Natural. In Nature there is all the raw material to make up human society if man so wishes but Nature itself is not social. Just as Nature has the materials needed to create the atomic bomb but Nature by itself is not an atomic bomb. By itself Nature does not allow for war, hunger, disease, inequality, injustice and oppression. Human society is as much a human invention as the steam engine. Human well-being is civilization's undertaken project; quite like the study project I had gone to Abujhmad with, that had to eventually drop. Ignorant Abujhmad did not speak of Truth, God or Enlightenment, or their later progenies like the State, democracy, justice and freedom. Like *vichaar* (thought) and *vyavahar* (action and behaviour), they are man-made and do not exist by themselves. Gradually my forgotten childhood village of the late '50s and '60s began coming back. At a rudimentary level, life there was not very different from that in Abujhmad, nor was different its ease with its small self.

2

State and the Simpleton

'Anyone who lives within their means suffers from a lack of imagination.'

—Oscar Wilde

THE majority of elders in my childhood village were illiterate. They had neither read of things nor, in most cases, seen or heard. In neither elders nor youngsters was there a noticeable inclination to ponder, discuss, read or write. Something of the village kept them at the margins, even outside.

There was no equivalent word for 'imagination' in our vocabulary and conversations. I remember people as hardly imaginative. By today's yardsticks both people and vocabulary seemed disinterested and dull. Not only were conversations and vocabulary such, we also did not have the cognitive infrastructure and equipment to foster imagination. Nor were they cultivated as some matter of design for life. Imagination cannot be without its nesting grounds. It needs grounds that spur it on. People would go through daily living—even work, quarrels, fun and laughter—with a bovineness. Our homes, trees, cattle, fields, skies, trails, canals, ponds, veerans and cremation or burial grounds too were reflective of the same bovineness.

In our fields, about two kilometres from home, was a little well of sweet and cold water. It was in the shade of the dense foliage of four *sheesham* (rosewood) trees and a *shahtoot* (mulberry) tree. Drawing the well's waters we would quench ourselves on hot afternoons with a good deal of coolness and sweetness. The hotter the day, the colder and sweeter the water, that is how it was. In winter, the water came lukewarm. Having sated our thirst, we would peep into the well's dark and narrow circumference at the waters beneath. Mirrors had not yet become common in our households, only a broken piece or two were to be found, that too often borrowed by some neighbour or the other. If one was available, it often lay forever untraceable amongst the thirty or forty people that made up our household for we were joint families. Mirrors had not yet become important to our daily lives. But in the dark of the little well we peered into was reflected clear as crystal our faces along with a few leaves, strands of grass, a frog or two and the circular sky. In due course of life and growing up in towns and cities we forgot what peeping was about.

People would spend long hours sitting by the well under the dense shade, nibbling at mulberries, or occasionally napping till the hot afternoon passed. Lifetimes were spent thus. There was also a small *dahana* (water channel) that strolled along and irrigated our fields. The elderly *barad* (banyan) tree was probably the most-drowsy one in the kheda—a vast and empty space. Sometimes cattle were tethered under its vast shade. Else it remained unoccupied. We would make little bullocks and carts from the barad's sturdy leaves. None knew how the barren reti of sand dunes came to sit by our fertile lands or since how long, nor did it occur to the village to find out. We did not enter the reti for it was a veeran. Veerans were not violated. They were the dwellings of desolation and forlornness for without such life could not be. One's own life too needs an appropriate degree of veeran. Human presence and footprint were to be kept small and humble. The reti was not brought under the plough. In fact, none brought anything under the plough except the small, scattered fields cultivated from habit and routine over generations without question or doubt. Generations had been lost to memory but not their ways of keeping one's presence small. Left fallow, the fields were ploughed every alternate year. The scattered and unconsolidated little fields gave our little needs more than we required to eat and wear the year round.

There being little interaction with other villages, we heard only infrequently of them or the world outside. People visited neighbouring villages to watch wrestling bouts or visit fairs once or twice a year. Most did not step beyond their own village or at the most those nearby. We heard anecdotes from those who went on foot or on donkeys to visit their daughters, sisters or aunts carrying gifts during festivals. Anecdotes were of great value and education. A bicycle or two was just beginning to reach the village. It was called the 'mechanical horse'. On a tiny road about three kilometres away ran the few buses and *tongas* (horse-drawn carriages) adorned with much embellishments. Buses were rarely utilized. I later found that in Bastar people hardly travelled and were not used to reaching their destinations quickly. The elderly and almost blind Aja walked for three days through dense forests, hills, valleys and rivers from Phulpur to his own village Khasgaon instead of choosing to reach in three hours by travelling in a jeep with me. 'Speed,' he had said, 'will cause me illness.'

Once in a blue moon we would walk to *Sahib ka Baag* (Sahib's orchard), four kilometres away in Saunti village. It was also called 'Saunti Wala Baag' (orchard at Saunti). It had once belonged to an Englishman. As far as I know, upon leaving India in 1947, the Englishman had given away the orchard to someone who lived in the town. On the dusty pathway to the Baag stood stunted trees of uncanny shapes, spreads and silences whose likes I later came to see in *Chandamama* (a fortnightly of fairy and mythological tales for adults and children) upon reaching the city and even later in Abujhmad. These trees were not tall but had very twisted, coiled and twined branches as though concealing something within. The Baag itself was spread over several acres. It was much too big for our small frameworks of daily living. Despite being there for a very long time, our village did not envisage having one such orchard of its own. There were many species of fruit trees in the Baag; we had nothing in the village as large or varied as those. There were caretakers who ensured that nobody plucked the fruits in the Baag. Fruits were sent twelve kilometres away to the market town of Baraut. In the village, we talked about its size, of the hundreds of trees, and that it once belonged to a white sahib. There came to be associated with it many stories, some of which were self-contradictory (what else are stories if they do not contradict or sidestep themselves, too). Many narrated these stories and many enjoyed them. The manners and flavours of telling were quite the same as those of stories they told from the epics. Some things had apparently stayed still over time.

We would frequently go to our own small baag of fifteen or twenty trees across the Big Canal. The baag was on another canal called the Small Canal. Big Canal was at the immediate periphery of our village. Adults, children and cattle would go there for baths and fun. The Small Canal was at a distance. The baag, was mostly of mango trees, with one or two of lemon and guava. The orchard provided enough fruit for our joint family, neighbours or others who did not have orchards, and even for the occasional passersby. All orchards in the village were thus. Grandfather would stay in our orchard day and night in the season of fruits. He was there mostly to irrigate the trees with jaggery-mixed water once a week. The baag was shaded and quiet. Grandfather would spend the fruit season there smoking his *hukka* (hookah) and keeping the fire alive, for it was needed for his next smoke. Matchboxes had still not come into use in the village and fire was preserved under the ash for when it was needed next. Grandfather also had to shoo the birds away lest they spoil the fruits. However, neither did his shooing work nor did they stay away. He was the same with us children, chasing us away. Mangoes were aplenty and, laden with the weight, the branches would nearly touch the ground. We could pluck the ripe ones or pick up those that had fallen but not those that were still raw. Lying on the hemp cot, the gurgling hukka pipe in his mouth, he, like with the avian creatures, kept an eye on us children too but equally unsuccessfully. Climbing the trees was permitted only if we wanted to play jumping from the branches into the fulsome waters of the Small Canal that flowed adjacent.

For around three or four months of the year this was what grandfather did. For the remaining year, he sat on the cot at home, ate and slept. Or he would take a round of the fields in the evenings to see how his youngsters and lands were doing. And he smoked the hukka continuously. He also met up with friends and scolded the youngsters of the family, neighbourhood and village. He was feared for his strictness. Only grandmother stood up to him. Of course, little girls of the family and neighbourhood would scold him back when, while playing, they were asked to not disturb his afternoon nap. It was rather rare, however, that girls were scolded.

When life is simple and ordinary, there is little or no discomfort. Elderly Bulki used to say no sin could come to Abujhmad.

A deep fondness and respect for ancestors was shared across families in the neighbourhood. A family would often recount the names of not only its own ancestors but also those of the other families. Over time ancestors had become shared and common. Many anecdotes would be recounted from their lives. They were our legends, heroes and heroines. Like our small gods and goddesses, ancestors were small too. They could be anyone: from an aunt of long ago married into another village to a deceased uncle in the neighbour's family. Larger than life legends from history, mythology or elsewhere stayed at the periphery of our conversations and chitchats. Whereas gods and goddesses were occasionally the butt of village jokes, the legends, heroes and heroines were not. Ancestors were sufficient for our small lives and needs. Whether material, mythological or conceptual, our nearest was not dispensed away in favour of the farthest. Everything came from the family, neighbourhood or village. Later, I found the same in Bastar and other regions.

Though there was the sacrosanct to memory but, depending on the narrating elder, so were there many additions and subtractions, many fluctuations, deflections and swerves in the anecdote or story. Such is folk memory and its recalling. It is not cast in stone. Facts were important but memory wandered outside the frameworks of factual narratives. Facts were not overriding, only underlying. That which was being recalled did not have to be listened to attentively. Nevertheless, over time, it sank into the listener and, processed by his or her own internal persona, was recounted at another point in time to another group of listeners. The narrating elder, in his or her own way, would thus give our heroes back to us with a swerve here and a lurch there. Like the few stories from epics, the tellings of our elders had many variations, yet quintessentially stayed the same. When *The Arabian Nights*, telling some of the noblest and most magical of stories, travelled to India over distances, times, and cultures, it underwent many transformations in nuances and effects without altering the spirit and tonality.

Life was slow, undemanding and available in its tiny little ways and satisfactions. What was, as it was, was nurtured. There was not the modulation of what the village landscape brought to our lives—smallness, stillness, ease and bovineness. Living, thus, was *Dharm*—the way and conduct of life. Later, I found strong and palpable similarities in Bastar, where had begun the revisits to memories of my childhood village.

Not much was needed for simple and ineffectual lives. People did not have to be somewhere or make something out of themselves.

Such ways have been common to the adivasi and folk communities of India, and probably amongst such communities the world over. Neither cognitive infrastructure and equipment nor their by-products imagination, intelligence or other forms of cleverness were needed from outside as aids to living. The village stayed within its intrinsic nativity, memory, geography, thought and speech. We were not to violate the intrinsic given by our landscape. Virtue and Truth become necessary when a whole society, having subverted itself, is unable to endure its constructs and subversions caused by transgressing the landscapes, svabhav and dispositions. I began my education in the village *madrasa* (an Arabic word for school, not necessarily religious). However, later when I came to the city school there was the subject called 'moral science'. It continued till standard five; and in one way or the other, in higher classes too. In the village we did not need to learn morals and values in the madrasa.

Just as in Bastar, in our village we did not have an omnipotent God but there were several deities. The Supreme God, who lives in Heaven, and Its corollaries of Virtue and Truth came from outside when the Green Revolution came in the 1960s; consolidation of small and scattered landholdings into large fields of documented ownership (as against of verbal consensus); felling of orchards; erosion of mounds of dung as manure; schools and formal education; aspirations; pondering; discussion and contemplation. There also came books and literature that seemed concerned with giving meaning and effect to our lives. All of these came more or less together. They brought along a lot else, too. Much of it is too subtle to be counted and listed down. Except succumbing to these external arrivals, the bovine village did not know how to deal with them or itself. With our small orchards felled for the plough, Sahib ka Baag became the emblem of good lives, profitable economy, non-bovine and efficient ways of being on earth. Water bodies were done away with and ponds filled up to build houses. The traditional Persian wheels and the idling ambiance they invoked fell in disuse with the coming of mechanized irrigation. Desolation and forlornness of the python-like reti was brought under the tractor. Guests came no more, or at least did not seem like guests who used to come only a while earlier. An away road upon which plied the few buses and trucks now passed in hordes through the village. Sitting by the little well under the dense shade of the four sheesham trees, its cold and sweet water and the nearby channel was deemed unproductive. Joint families wilted and disappeared. Neighbours were no longer family. Adults or children, it was a neurotic phase for all. It continues to this day. Grandfather suffered neglect in the family and neighbourhood, and passed away. My father was transferred from Kashmir to a family station. Mother and us children left to be with him.

By and by I learnt. I learnt of the scale and size of contemporary living, its own peculiar phenomenon and things that make it needlessly larger than life. Habitations are large, distances are large, ideas and concepts are large, human reach and accomplishments are large; the world is large; and the cosmos is immeasurably large. Human presence and footprint is now unprecedentedly large. There is practically nothing any more that is as small as the life given to us.

Eventually, it began to be said that largeness dwells within the small. How deeply deceiving that was!

But, more importantly, for me it led to revisiting my illiterate elders, their small reach, small landscape and small lives. Their unimaginative bovineness does not lend itself to recounting by my literacy, vocabulary, imagination and the language they craft together.

I have revisited my native village innumerable times but could never regain it. Now shadows linger within. Instead of bovineness we got pulled into the stirred and the futile.

3

Outside the Doorframe

It had rained more that night. There was water under my feet and the earth was slippery. There being no furniture other than my own haunches, I was sitting on them. Outside the doorframe stood ominously the stump of that tree; the one that had been burnt by lightning four years ago. I could not see it in the dark; but it had always stood there as my nearest companion. A damp and warm wind blew through the thousand little crevices in the bamboo-strip walls of the hut. It was an old night; how old, I could not have known. So old that it passed through bones and being. The hills, skies, trees, rivers and anthills were old. All were old since, what seemed, the very beginning. Some phenomena or ages remain indeterminate. They defy an outsider's yardsticks of living; in fact, they defy living itself. The deeply buried within, since times immemorial, stays unknown. It may not be described.

Each night was so; each without sound or syllable. Yet, it was almost the only experience that was heard and seen. I often felt that nights here in Abujhmad are a different kingdom that have to be dwelled in after sunset. In some strange way, nights here side-step the sense of being a human; and all that affirms the human. Never harmful, they were at the same time like a foreboding. Days were better but no less ominous. The forms that appeared of the thick and intertwined vegetation with the coming of the sun, even though seemingly magical, were as ominous as the nights that swallowed them. Yet, in the dark of the night, I waited for the sun and the forms to reappear. It was not easy being without forms—even one's own—in that darkness when one oneself becomes the darkness. With something of an adolescent's awkwardness, the sun, when it came, did make a difference. It brought a degree of comfort but there still was to it some measure of that which a rank outsider may not be fully at home with. That fullness of phenomenon and stir that the eyes and ears mingle and engage with ceaselessly was haywire if not amiss. There was little or nothing to respond to or engage with. What response does one make, if at all, to the continued stillness and silence? Or to the intertwined trees, creepers and bushes which stood as though frozen in time? Often one felt one lived under the shadow of unuttered something that was continuously on the verge of speaking but never did.

That night, it had rained more than the other nights. It had drizzled for many long hours and water had accumulated under my feet. The earth had become slippery. Outside the doorframe stood ominously the stump of that old tree. Huts in Abujhmad had doorframes but no doors to shut or open. So the doorframe of my hut was open. No animal would have walked in, certainly not the troublemaker bear. Animals do not like being wet or have water under the paws, nor do they like to walk on slippery earth.

Most of the monsoon months there was the lightest of drizzles. Early rain was like a mist. It hung on for many days. One could neither hear nor see it falling nor could one feel it on the bare body and limbs; the rain showed itself only when everything gradually felt damp and covered in lightly running minuscule droplets. Or when the grass, plants and shrubs dampened one's legs and arms; when they brushed against them did one know it was raining. Rain was as unperceived by the body as daylight or the dark. I would cover myself with a sihadi leaf. A single leaf is large enough to cover almost all of the human body.

On such nights, many nocturnal insects hovered around the eyes. I could sense them in the dark just as they did me, and my companion tree that stood outside the doorframe.

4

Barber's Tales

By the large dirty-water drain is a barber shop in the village of Shahberi near where I now live in Ghaziabad district, Uttar Pradesh. It is a small shop of three weary- and fatigued-looking chairs and three similar barbers. Ever since I began living here, some ten years ago, I have been visiting the shop for haircuts and beard trims. A good-hearted acquaintance naturally develops over time between strangers who see each other frequently; so it has been with the barbers and me. They greet me with 'asalam-wa-leikum' and I greet back 'wa-leikum-asalam'. The older man at the shop is a good tattler of tales behind people's backs. 'The one who left just now with the "Muslim cut" to his beard is not a good Muslim. He skips namaz all five times a day; he is a Muslim only in beard and attire. I have never seen that other one at the mosque for *jumme ki namaz* (Friday prayers). Nor do most who come here keep the *roza* (fast). They are all fake but pretend to be pious. Under the burqas their women wear trousers, shirts and lipstick; and they think nobody knows, that everybody is a fool. Many splurge on alcohol but fight when it comes to paying for my services here. Muslims here no longer heed the Nabi (Prophet Muhammad). They are bogus.' He goes on tattling thus while glancing now and then at the Bollywood films of ostentatious actors, which many times border on vulgarity, on the small television while occasionally humming their love songs. A picture of the Holy Ka'ba hangs above the television. Himself beardless, he almost always politely insists on giving my beard the 'Muslim cut' and every time I decline with similar politeness. It is ever a tiny struggle when both want to have their own way. Sure enough, my 'non-Muslim cut' must be adding to his repository of tales despite his virtuous displays of deference towards me.

There is a strange, almost endearing, ambiguity, if not inconsistency, to him and his ways.

In my childhood village house, our main door opened into the street. At a height of about ten feet from the floor was a mirror above the door. Weather beaten, it had become tarnished over time. To this day, I have not understood what its ostensive purpose was. Who would look into a mirror ten feet high and set above a door that opened into the street? And that too a hazy one. One of the few visitors of the mirror was a swinging sparrow that came several times during the day. Fluttering its wings and chirping angrily all the while, it kept quarrelling with its reflection. This had caused several scratches of its little beak and claws on the mirror.

The door's two swinging halves were oiled about twice a year for strength, longevity and gloss. We used mustard oil extracted from the crop we grew in our fields. The door hinges were also oiled for easy closing and opening. There was much dust at the hinges and right underneath the two halves where they touched the earthen floor. Heavy as the doors were, they had become quite stuck in the floor and at the hinges. Whereas the rest of the household was swept every day and paved with dung on alternate days, why the hinges and the bottom of the doors were not swept and cleaned I do not know. Because of accumulated dust the doors could not be closed. So they remained open year after year. No one set them 'right'. If not for closing and opening, what the doors were for I do not know. Anyone or anything walked in—other people, dogs, cats, birds, winds, sounds, dust and the young buffaloes, cows and goats. It was so in every household. Locks from Aligarh were famous for their strength but, barring an exception or two, people did not use them to secure their smaller doors in the house. The locks were of coarse iron and would have been fretful for thieves, though there was not much thieving. But stealing of cattle and other livestock was quite common.

Years later, and much removed from my village in time and space, I saw that the Abujhmadia huts had no doors. There were doorframes but no doors to open or shut. Winds, gods, spirits, wild animals, space and time were free to come and cohabit with humans in the tiny huts. When the little village of three or four huts was cut off from everything during the monsoons, its people would in a formal ceremony re-invite the cohabitants to return to the village; for without them Abujhmadia could not be.

Though in the care of shepherds, cattle in my childhood village were left free to roam. That made them easy targets for a certain community whose main livelihood and good reputation came from cattle stealing. Its people specialized in stealing and were known just as a good potter is known for making well-baked pots or a carpenter for sturdy cots. They came from the surrounding villages of infertile lands; and were sometimes feared—along with being shown a hint of regard—for their daredevilry and bold ways.

However, the stealing of cattle was not stealing as we understand it now. Stealing would be, say, as in the case of a gold or silver ornament, which there wasn't much of in any case. Cattle stealing was something *like* stealing, something a little short of the act; something that lay between stealing and non-stealing, of a blur where both were possible. While there was a social frowning upon and disapproval of this community's ways as such, there also seemed to be a consent. The more they were adept at stealing, the more well-reputed the boys became in their community and the more eligible for marriage.

We called this particular community by a name popularly prevalent in the region. But it was a twisted version of their name in Hindi. People in our region were famous for twisting names and identities of one and all in funny ways. We preferred oblique references as opposed to direct ones. It was as if names and identities of gods, men and phenomenon ought to be only suggestive of something else that was unknown to us. The greater part of everyday living was deliberately tangential and ambiguous; inexplicit and of a certain evasiveness. There was something metaphorical to such speech and living—as though the reference was to something unknown and wordless. People, however, were not uncomfortable inhabiting this space. Our dialect, like all dialects, was thus metaphorical and nebulous. The native gods and goddesses looking after our crops, health and well-being were addressed similarly. Hindus and Muslims were, in today's lexicon, separate people. But the native deities were for all. When it came to deities everyone became the same. So did people become the same in their dialect, clothing, habits, facial expressions and gait. My avowedly vegetarian and older cousins and other youngsters would steal in the dark of night to a so-called *malech* (untouchable or of impure conduct) Suleman *chacha's* (uncle's) house and savour mutton on Eid (non-vegetarian food was forbidden amongst Hindus). Chacha was a so-called 'malech' as well as a loved and respected 'chacha' simultaneously. He knew and affectionately cooked that much extra mutton on the auspicious day. All elders knew of the boys' eagerness for the change of palate for that night. There was much tacit consent of their behaviour and only a slight outward frown. There were boundaries but they could be stealthily crossed back and forth. Such was the framework of lives—much vitality lived in stealth and darkness, much play that kept the village same and together.

Sociologists and anthropologists say cattle stealing, even though 'criminal', was a way of balancing wealth and power in the region. I cannot say either way. There were not many of the other kinds of thieves because not many valuables or goods existed in our houses. The region's material culture, as in folk or adivasi cultures elsewhere, was such. Cattle was prized more.

Lower down in what is called the social hierarchy, the village barber was always the barber; he was only a notch above the skinner of dead animals and maker of footwear. But the barber was also the designated fixer of sanctimonious marriages; he was skilled at it and took pride as such. The older women of the households, particularly, would coax and pamper him to find a good bride or groom for the young in the family. Having lived together over generations, he had full knowledge of his host family. Around the wedding season, he would walk to other villages far and near looking for prospective brides and grooms for others' children just as he would for his own. Like the *Bhaat* (keeper of genealogical records and other details), he had his contacts and detailed information. His recommendations had a key role in finalizing matches. When it came to his own daughter's marriage, the host families (each barber acquired several over generations) would begin to contribute from days ahead of the ceremony wheat, lentils, rice, milk, curd, butter, buttermilk, clarified butter, cots and earthen pots (cash was in very little usage; most transactions were in kind) for the marriage party that stayed for three days. The barber's daughter was the daughter of the village.

My elder uncle's bosom friend was a Muslim man from the village Sara (also known as Asara). Though they never ate from each other's pots and pans they always remained avowedly the best of friends. They were more like brothers—the idea of a 'friend' had just about begun creeping into our vocabulary and was still somewhat alien. I first read of it in schoolbooks in the city. Such brotherhood as my uncle and his friend's was not uncommon. Uncle's friend played a key role in some affairs of our family, particularly the marital. Once when uncle and my cousins (his sons) quarrelled, he left home with his own hukka, *thaali* (plate) and *lota* (rounded brass jar for drinking water), and walked the ten or so kilometres to the Muslim friend's house to sulk and tattle against the sons. After three or four months, the repentant sons and an elder or two went and cajoled him back home; but only after receiving a severe reprimand from the friend. On the other hand, unlike with Muslims, though we could eat with the Brahmin, the Brahmin was practically looked down upon by almost all communities. Brahmins were discouraged from coming and settling in the village. Our village had only one Brahmin, Indu. A more or less similar ratio prevailed in other villages. Like the *baniya* (trader) or the unmaintained and dysfunctional temple and mosque, Indu was ever the butt of jokes. Brahmins were looked down on for they did not engage with land, agriculture or associated activities in any notable way. One so disengaged had to be a pariah. Their only function was conducting wedding rituals and performing the occasional *havans* (semi-religious ceremonies to purify homes against the evil and harmful) in a family. There were no notable ceremonies of birth or death for him to perform.

People lived more in community than in caste or religious distinctions. All communities such as the Jats, Rajputs, Muslims, Aheers, Gujars, scavengers of cattle dung, which was used as manure and for covering earthen floors—there being no human scavenging as households did not have toilets; scavenging in many cases was done by the families too—blacksmiths, carpenters, oil pressers, weavers and potters had a collective and common measure of good reputation, but also had it in their own respective communities.

To turn the blind eye is to actually see. The nebulous alone sees. Only the none—the uncertain, inexact and indeterminate can see. People echoed such worldviews and ways in their everyday lives, vocabularies and interactions. Then none can see and, hence, know the way we now see and know the same phenomena. One cannot see the one, nor many the one. The seer is the none, for it has turned the blind eye; for the seer is of the uncertain, inexact and indeterminate. Then none sees the none in all its resplendence. It alone is none with itself. The none alone is the self of the none. Those who 'see' are with the un-self; the one, many and countless. The none does not know the un-self; neither the one nor countless. The moment one sees without turning the blind eye, one is irrevocably on the path to the countable, clarified and explicit; certain, exact and determinate. The village kept at a distance from that.

When social-political scientists, economists and other experts began to take interest in our region, the relative blur and nebulousness amongst castes, communities and religions began to be erased and things started becoming distinct, neatly segmented and established. In spite of their noblest intentions the fact remained that the experts were neither born here nor brought up in our ways; nor did they have any other living association with us. Just that, ironically, their profession happened to be that of studying and researching villages and regions that were not their own; just as Abujhmad was not my own when I had gone to study it. My village was, and is, for them no more than an entity like any other entity without heartbeats. They began categorizing its communities and their relationships into neat sections and sub-sections, which were sometimes understated, at times exaggerated and sometimes even fabricated. The Jats, Rajputs, Muslims, Aheers, Gujars, scavengers of dung, blacksmiths, carpenters, oil pressers, weavers and potters began acquiring sharp identities of their own as against the blurred and fluid one, the 'back and forth', that they had lived by over the centuries. Now we have different kinds of Hindus, Muslims, Aheers, Gujars, barbers and the rest; they are more of themselves than they were till even about forty years ago. There also began coming in the scriptural religions of sharp distinctions and divisiveness. Everything of our blurredness had now to be sharp, clinically defined and accordingly segmented. We began to be irrevocably tied to the modernizing and 'democratizing' State. This or that way, the social-political scientists, economists and other experts turned out to be representatives of the State narrative; and still continue to. The adivasi of Bastar and elsewhere is undergoing the same fate. Furthermore, he or she does not understand them even though they are speaking about him or her. After the mass conversions at Meenakshipuram[1] in 1981, the Hindus of my native village felt threatened by the Muslims and renovated the old and abandoned temple into the kind that temples are —of ostentation, worship and rituals. Indu was brought out of the folds to became our first priest in living memory. After four or five months, however, he was beaten up for the noise and fanfare that temple worship entails. He had to temporarily run away to another village. Old ways are not easy to do away with. By and by, however, those ways have now withered.

In a farmer, barber, blacksmith or potter's experience of many generations, land itself is a religion. That is where beliefs, values and gods came from. The religion of scriptures may not compare with it. Scriptural religion was often derided as a kind of vulgar conspicuousness but still taken some note of—like the aforesaid television in the barber's shop. Like waters, winds and veerans, lands have their own temperaments, mutualities and ethos. This or that way, everyone engaged with land and lived by it. Now we, like the experts, live by purchasing power.

I cannot say much about community, caste or religious configurations in the rest of the country. Perhaps things have been different there. India is so vast, old and multi-layered that I could not have hoped to know it more than a little nor belong to it in the same way as I do to the region of my birth and ancestry. With the exception of Bastar and the village of my childhood, I have not had a long and personal association with other regions of India.

There is something of the old blur about my acquaintance, the barber, in the village of Shahberi. People still go to him

---

1 *Mass-Conversions of Meenakshipuram—A Sociological Enquiry* by Mumtaz Ali Khan, University of Michigan, 1983, and several other books and news reports of that era. Since 1981 it has been a well-known fact across India.

despite being tattled about. I guess that is the case with me too, even though he had once clipped the bottom of my earlobe while cutting my hair and stealing a glance at the actors on his television. Extremely apologetic, albeit in a flamboyant manner, he had cured the wound by inserting a flaming matchstick into the small gash. I could barely suppress a shriek. But the flame had stopped the bleeding.

5

Ten Feet of the World

MUCH about the wild is innately gentle and well-behaved. No wonder the Abujhmadia is its near perfect mimic; as are the animals, other creatures and non-creatures. They are shy and almost never cross the limits of clean behaviour and conduct. A tiger is far too shy to easily show itself. It prefers to walk away from trails; so do leopards, wild boars, bison, snakes and scorpions. Humans stick to walking only on trails unless looking for a cow killed by a tiger or leopard in the thickets. Marauding tigers and leopards chasing after humans are of those steeped in sanitized lives.

Over thirty-five years have gone by since I left Abujhmad in 1985 and began staying in its adjoining areas in Bastar. Ever since, however, Abujhmad has continued to churn in me. Though I have been writing of it for about the past nine years, I still find it indescribable. I do not know where to begin or where to end, or even how or what to write. No matter how much or how little I have written of it, I am yet to find the words that that are its own.

Just as I cannot evoke Abujhmad, neither can I say what the people there were about. Or if they had what is called a view of themselves or the world. Or how they understood life and living. I do not know if my companion of every night, the tree stump that stood across the doorframe of my hut and who, I had invested with much during those nights, or if the tiger in the bamboo cluster had a worldview, or whether they considered it even worth it to have one. If it can be called so at all, the Abujhmadias' was the smallest of worlds, one that leaves no footprint or trace. They knew of very little outside the tiny village of three–four scattered huts. Or, at the most, knew of some neighbouring villages five or six kilometres away which they visited no more than once or twice in a lifetime. Or they knew of the few obscure trails that led through the nearby forested hills yet deeper into the region. But no more. What view to have then? Having a view or understanding would be akin to making unkind noises; just as we in the outside world do. The learned may describe it in several ways while they, the Abujhmadias, did not have even a word for it.

There is much that the region alludes to. Over time I found there is also much that alludes to it in turn. Abujhmad is everywhere. It is a metaphor for good and sane living.

The two little boys, the little girl and their ten goats dwell somewhere in the village of Shahberi near where I now live. After the day's grazing and wandering, they and their goats are racing back home heedlessly, rather recklessly, in complete abandon. Little swirls of dust, bleats, little hooves, small feet and laughter mingle in togetherness with the earth. They seem not so many but one and the same.

The dusty goats run homeward uncontrollably fast over the small slope. The slope is about ten feet of incline. Depending on which direction I am coming from, I climb up or down during my evening walks. It is immediately next to the dirty-water drain that was once a small canal of earthen banks. Its thick and blackish water is barely visible under heaps of plastic and other sundry refuse. As the goats run down in un-reined freedom, bleating and flailing the hind legs randomly, they are followed in unison by the three goatherds—the two dusty little boys and the equally dusty little girl of two dusty ponytails and threadbare red ribbons. In themselves, they are all about the ten feet of slope; not to be lost for anything. The world for them is no more than the ten feet. All is invested and put at stake, as if the repay, and more, is guaranteed. The little girl of dusty hair and red ribbons rushes past me like a hurricane, brushing me and endangering both of us on the little slope. I mock-scold her, 'Should you be running so fast and dangerously?' Oblivious, given over completely to the slope and short of breath in the small lungs, she yells vehemently, 'No, I am not running,' and continues the wanton pace and spirit till all disappear over the dusty small bridge across the dirty small drain.

They require just a small portion of the earth. Their footprint is small. This is the goats' and goatherds' evening ritual of strange solemnity every day. Such revitalize stillness and stir without utterance. There is again that which I fail to put my finger on—that very same of the endless and senseless, indeed all of Abujhmad's unuttered. It may not be evoked.

Existence is ever kind when left alone. Game plays the game.

6

There Showed a Tree

THERE is a tree. Today it showed itself.
   There is a tree. It stands near my house. It has stood there for years. I pass by it every day. Today it showed up.
   So today I saw the tree. It stands by the wayside but today it showed itself. A forlorn-looking mound of earth sits in its shade. I go back seven decades when, under the dense foliage of a shahtoot and four sheesham trees, was a small well a little outside the childhood village. The well's waters stay in me as do the foliage and shade. On the forlorn mound sit drowsily four dogs of unoccupied freedom just as we did under the trees. Two are barking half-heartedly, without a purpose, providing themselves amusement in the day's dull heat. It is too hot and wearisome to run around and play. The third is a half yelp, like a disinterested agreement with the half-hearted barks. As though the yelp just happened to be as happened to be the disinterest

and agreement; like the whiff of wind that just happened to turn a curve, or the pebble that just happened to lie on the ground. Generations of humans and desolation just happened to be as did the village of a shahtoot and four sheesham trees some decades ago; but still continue to stay in me. There is a fulsome yawn after the dog's half yelp and its ears go back as do my seventy years; for life and love happen in a yawn when wakefulness is and is not. When there cohabit inertia and bovineness. The preoccupied neither yawn nor love; nor do those wanting to be somewhere other than themselves. The town is of the preoccupied; desolation is of the inert and poised. There is a veeran buried under this town. Dogs know this; so do the mound and the tree. The fourth sits quietly like the sage. It is like the tree that stands above the mound or those at the small well whose waters stay in me.

Today I saw the tree. It stands like the spoilt idler. It must have stood similarly that day when the earth was small and humans lived in the outside; as humans and animals of Abujhmad still do. Or like the mound atop which sit four idling dogs; or the shahtoot and sheesham that still caress me.

It is not possible to live without forgetfulness and sleep. Landscapes and cultures too need sleep. Our past has been of sleep, restfulness and poise. Those that do not sleep are doomed to impairment. For, then is caused language, society, friendship and the State. These are of continuous and eternal vigilance and wakefulness, of recitation and remembrance. They are of the striving and toiling; of those that are everywhere but at themselves. Such are the homeless victims and carriers of the State. Such are their towns and cities buried under which lie the vast vacant veerans.

Today I saw the tree. Its desolation forges a temper, a svabhav, of delicate absences and dissolutions; the dissolution of sums and totals in a world contingent upon ceaseless activity and growth. Desolation forges a disposition to live without a vocabulary of speech and speed, of the one and many of mathematics.

More than the 'thing', the 'nothing' was integral to life. Life ought not be full and inhabited. Footprints ought to be small. The veeran lived in every nook and crevice. It lived in the absence of activity and aspiration. Much happened in absence, like life's liveliness and vitality. Spaces were earmarked in houses and neighbourhoods for the nothing and veeran to be.

There was the reti, the stretch of sand dunes, in my childhood village. It lay at the edge of lush green agricultural fields and stretched a kilometre or two. How the mounds of sands came to be right next to well-irrigated and fertile lands, one does not know. But it was next to our fields with their small well and trees of foliage and shade. We saw them every day, the reti, the well and the trees. Whereas the reti beckoned, none dared go. The reti was infertile and without any beneficial use, but it was allowed to be. It lent us the pull of vacancy. On its small mounds of sands grew bulrush, extreme solitude and silences. Several generations had lived without stepping into the reti. Village dogs that ran the three or so kilometres to harass the monkeys at Bangla on the Big Canal, skirted its sides. Even the robber chose the sugarcane fields to hide in instead of the secluded reti.

These are what crafted the village, its svabhav, vocabulary and speech of every day. That is what its life was—of avoidances and evasions, of hiding and seeking. Of the incontrovertibly implicit. Like that of a sage. Like the dogs atop the forlorn mound. It was the absence of aspiration, inclination and transgression. That is how it was.

7

Gender Relations in the Wilds

Sometime in 2017, a magazine from Pune suggested I write on the, 'Status of women in Abujhmad' for its Diwali issue. They sent a set of questions on which the write-up was to be based. The exercise felt odd to me because that is not how Abujhmad may be sensed and spoken of. Nevertheless, it felt like an opportunity to write about the region to a wider readership.

Like other old societies, Abujhmad has very few issues and concerns to contend with. It is simple and bare. Man-made arrangements, institutions, notions and concepts are few or unknown. Of animals, rivers, hills, mysteries, stillness, expanses, sky and space, it is a region of innate mutuality and reciprocity. These determine the pace and rhythm of how humans ought to live and relate if they are to survive contentedly. Viewed from Abujhmad, an exclusively human society is an artificial construct whose gender or other relationships are contrived and disproportionate. Modern societies ask questions of the region, for example, what is the status of women in Abujhmad? Such questions can come only from a community exclusively of humans. Like other old communities elsewhere, Abujhmad does not ask questions or give answers. That is not its way. It will be unfair to view relationships there through a question–answer mode.

Problems occur when language interacts with dialect. The question comes from language and the answer is to be provided by dialect, which very rarely asks a question or gives an answer. Two different, often opposite, sensibilities and values enter into communication. A certain question may not exist in one while it may in the other. Take for example the question, 'How are you?' People in Abujhmad do not ask such questions; nor did they in my village of childhood. To formulate answers from one according to the requirements of the other will not be just. Often there came the impression that the Abujhmadia experiences a difficulty in formulating questions, as though they have had to come out of their skin. Usually, after asking my name they did not know what else to ask. None ever asked why I had come to Abujhmad or what I did in Delhi. But even after forty years, Delhi still asks, 'What did you do in Abujhmad? Why did you go there?'

On the issue of the relationship between women and men, too, it will only be fair to see Abujhmad through its own eyes. If a certain issue does not exist, it is a judgement on one asking about it.

The questions sent by the magazine were direct (questions necessarily have to be that). On the other hand, there is nothing that is direct in the wild. It would have been inappropriate to dismiss or belittle the magazine's questions. So, I shuffled the order in which they were placed. I also had to dull the sharpness of some. A handful, I am afraid, had to be put aside completely. Given the context in which Abujhmad's women and men live, the article may not have answered the questions as well and as sharply as it was expected to. But I hoped it would give some intimation of the answers that reflected the Abujhmadia experience. Abujhmad itself is an intimation and impression of something inscrutable.

Broadly, adivasis can be divided into two groups: first, those who are in the mainstream of contemporary life. Modernity and its arrangements have made substantial inroads into them. Second, those who are pre-modern or primitive and stay outside man-made arrangements, processes, institutions and practices.

As in other primitive communities, human needs come from, and are provided for, by culture and arrangements of the wilds. That renders human endeavour that much more needless. Food, shelter, medicine, mutuality, recreation and such necessities are already there when one is born. No more is needed for the rest of one's life. There is not the hunger or lingering disease, nor molestation, rape, violence, inequality, crime or injustice, which the outside world is both creating and fighting against continually. In Abujhmad, I never came across or heard of crimes against women, not even of teasing or other manifestations of maladjusted societies.

Before speaking of the woman–man relationship in the region, it is significant to understand that Abujhmad, per se, does not distinguish between the human and the wild landscape. The village of three or four huts is situated in the wild, and the wild in the village. One without the other will not be. Both are continually traversing in and out of each other. Hence tigers, leopards, bears, bison, snakes, ghosts, ancestors and spirits keep walking in and out of the tiny village and the village keeps going into 'their territory', as does the vegetation, rocks and immense anthills. The small thatch-and-bamboo huts are of the same irregular design and architecture as the surrounding wild. In that vegetation it is not easy to recognize a tiger even a few metres away where its contours and colours intermingle with the surroundings. Nor is it possible to recognize the Abujhmadia sitting amidst anthills, rocks and boulders nestling in thickets of vegetation, all overlaid by an endless canopy of ancient trees. One merges into another effortlessly and seem the same. All are naked. For the untrained eye, the contour, form, texture and hue of one does not appear noticeably different from the other. Just as the animal moves out of its cave or burrows for food, so does the human out of the tiny hut to gather root and shoot, seed and fruit, fish and crab, conviviality and sexual intimacy with the partner or spouse. Life happens outside the animal's small cave and the human's small hut. These impact relationships.

On an average day—the average is unchanging—the Abujhmadia's preoccupations are cooking, making leaf plates and cups, fetching water in a hollowed-out gourd from the stream or drinking there itself, getting the bamboo mat from inside the hut to the outside, distilling *mahua* (liquor made from mahua flowers), combing each other's hair and adorning with the occasional wildflower, singing and dancing, chatting and sleeping. Now and then, there is weaving a rope out of the sihadi vine, taking or giving haircuts with burning twigs, weaving a mat from bamboo strips, sharpening the knife, arrowhead or axe, weaving fish traps from vines and bamboo strips, looking for termites under the hut, or fetching the fish from the *tele* (bamboo trap). All these chores are done by both men and women (sometimes more by men). Catching wild rats for dinner is usually done by children, at times under adult supervision, for the rats are large. The natural differences between men and women, like childbearing and breastfeeding, are as they are. In no discernible way do they adversely impact women.

Food gathering takes place about twice or thrice a week. Whereas food is simple, cooking is simpler. Without oil or spices, it is elementary, either roasted or boiled, something that almost anybody can accomplish. Skinning the fish or animal or taking the shell off a crab is mostly done by men. Tasks are often interchanged, and men also do the roasting or boiling while women do the skinning and preparation or make leaf plates and cups. Cutting of vegetables is usually done by women. Leaf plates and cups are mostly made by children, occasionally participated in by both parents. When the woman is menstruating, all work is done by men and children.

Bringing up children—were one to use this expression—is as simple as cooking. There is not the looking after offspring as is known in the outside world. If one were to look at it from Abujhmad, parents have only a small role in the child's upbringing. Upbringing happens largely on its own. Just as the wilds, food, landscape and human life are intertwined, so is upbringing intertwined with them. It is more the wilds and community that brings up children. The child is not so much of its parents as of community and landscape. Breastfeeding by the mother happens for the first few months. When going out for food gathering, a child of four or five months (sometimes even younger) is left behind on a bamboo mat, where it is soon joined by other children—the puppies, kittens, goat kids, piglets and chickens as their parents too have gone out for food. All her or his life the Abujhmadia lives in such companionship and conviviality. As she or he grows the companionship is enlarged to include the vegetation, hills, rivers, animals, spirits and the sky. She or he does not consider themselves as separate from all this. None of the arrangements are man-made. Right from birth, Abujhmadias are one with their wilds as a dancer is with dance.

Life being simple and bare, the Abujhmadia circumvents much that has become integral to lives in the outside world. Let us take as an example, the taking of decisions. If decisions have to be taken, it is then a poor condition of life. When and whom to marry is not decided as such; either way it just happens between two lovers living in close neighbourhoods over the years. Family or others do not matter here; they know the girl or boy as much as the two know each other. When to have a child or how many is also not a decision between couples. Like upbringing and marriages, children happen on their own. Usually, a couple has two children, rarely three, but never did I come across one with more. An estimated 13,000,[2] the Abujhmadia population has been stable over the years. Boys and girls are brought up alike. Women wear a *lugga* (a short wrap around the waist) and men a loin cloth. The rest of the body remains bare. Often, the mother gives birth unaided and all by herself. Birthing takes place in a squatting position anywhere outside the hut. During or after childbirth, the new mother does not require assistance. Once the newborn arrives, she is up and about in no time and walks into the village carrying the child.

The temper of the wilds is such that it is virtually impossible to find people who choose to live alone as a loner, saint, monk

---

[2] Till about a decade ago this was the estimated figure. There had never been a census by the Indian state. Nor was there a map. In the early 2000s an aerial map was made for geological purposes (iron ore, etc.). When I lived there (1980–85) there was no presence of the Indian state, not even in the form of a hand pump or lamp post.

or ascetic. The region has not heard of them. Companionship between men and women and the rest is the very foundation of life even though interaction between them is much less compared to the world outside. Seeds of companionship are sown early. As mentioned earlier, an infant grows up in intimate surroundings with other human and animal children, in fact, more of the latter. Once a child is nine or ten years old, it is mandatory for them to sleep the night away from parents and with other small and older children in the *ghotul* (a large hut where youngsters assemble from dusk to dawn). Sleeping the night at the parental home is given up forever. At the ghotul, relationships happen without adult control or influence. Older girls and boys begin pairing up. Observing them, the smaller children learn of mutuality, reciprocity, emotional and physical relationships with the opposite gender without adult direction. No one is taught; learning happens on its own. There are no separate cubicles or screens in the ghotul for the couples. Whereas privacy is important, it is not deemed necessary. No intimacy is private enough. Monogamy for both the girl and boy is encouraged, but so is changing partners. Being possessive is frowned upon. In ghotuls in another part of Bastar, sleeping with the same partner for more than three consecutive nights is discouraged. Though mostly there are no incidences of pregnancies from these relationships, yet they occur sometimes. The unwed girl gives birth to her baby. She marries the child's father or someone else she chooses. The child belongs to the adopted father as much. That the child is born of its mother is sufficient. Such a child or mother are not looked down on. Barring a stubborn bear or troublesome ghost, none is looked down upon. Once married, a girl and a boy can no longer enter the ghotul. Wife and husband set up their own hut. The ghotul is ever for the unmarried youngsters alone.

When physical intimacy between wife and husband is insufficient, the two resort to divorce. Instances of sexual incompatibility are few but they are there. She speaks her mind without hesitation. Both sides are heard by the village elders (rarely exceeding two or three in a village). If, however, the husband is away, say to a fair or festival, ex parte divorce is granted to the wife. Her version alone is sufficient. She is free to remarry that instant onwards. Such express divorce is not granted to the husband; the wife has to be there to give her version, too. Marital breakdowns, though uncommon, happen mostly due to sexual incompatibility; there being hardly any other issue. Communion is very important in the wilds' order of things. I do not know of episodes of extramarital relations. Composition of wild nature being as they are, and villages so tiny, deviations are neither desired nor possible. Words like 'wife' and 'husband' are unknown. Also, in my native village of childhood in north India, these words were not in currency. The common modes of address were 'mother or father of so and so', 'man' or 'woman', or 'hailing from so-and-so village' (the latter was used in the case of women since as wives they came from other villages).

Ten to twelve years of communion in a ghotul decides the marital partners. When membership is small—it is usually seven to eight young and grown-up girls and boys—then marriage can take place with one from another village. The boy, known as lhamsena, from that village comes to the house of the girl and spends 'three seasons thrice' (that is, three years) with her and her family. He stays in the house and partakes in all the family's activities like cooking, fetching firewood, repairing or changing the thatch roof, food gathering and hunting and the occasional shifting cultivation. Nights are spent in the ghotul for both the girl and the lhamsena. Along with the girl, her parents too are assessing *his* suitability; but the final say is invariably the girl's;

there almost never being a dispute. Upon marriage, they are free to set up their own hut and family in the girl's village, the lhamsena's village or any other place they choose. Usually, it is the latter. However, finding a spouse outside the village is uncommon, so is the incidence of lhamsena.

Again, for reasons of companionship, if a widow is not old, she opts to remarry.

Knowledge of a woman's reproductive processes and cycles is sacred. It is not told to men for fear of contamination. Passed from mother to daughter, it forever remains with women alone. Such privacies are sacred.

It is worth knowing that the hut and its size, the family and its size, the village and its size, the distances between villages, the distances covered between sunrise and sunset are all small. Relationships with and visits to other villages are rare. There is practically no intermingling between the villages. It is one's own tiny village that matters. A woman's place in the family is actually her place in the village. In such tiny villages, questions as 'whether women or men have more power and influence' do not arise. Women and men have practically the same or overlapping tasks, with much of their time spent sitting idly or occasionally chatting. There is no division of property amongst them because there exists neither property, nor the notion or ownership. Apart from a bamboo mat, a bow and a few arrows, two or three knives, fishing sieves, a loin cloth or a lugga and a wooden comb adorning the hair, there exist no other assets.

Abujhmad is innately irreligious. One cannot live in the wilds and be religious or reverent of scriptures and God. Though there is no religion as we understand, religiosity, however, comes naturally here; it is a 'religion' that comes from the wilds and wilds alone. The region has no formal religion; nor does their vocabulary have an equivalent word for it. I cannot say whether they ought be called 'pagan' for the word comes from people who practice one or the other formal religion. Even though people live in the ways of monks and ascetics, there are no such nomenclatures. It may not be wrong to say that the region is a large and natural hermitage. Discriminations of the religious kind against women are not to be found. There is no omnipotent God. But there are several local goddesses and gods. They are mostly in the form of ancestors, spirits, animals, trees and others; very finite and earthly. Only a handful of rituals exist around them.

Nor are there temples as we know of them. Pieces of stones and wood put together at the village periphery, by the river, or under the sacred saja tree, make up the temple. During a festival, women, men and children sit under the tree while the shaman recites incantations invoking ancestors and spirits. Meanwhile all have leaf-cups of mahua. A goat, chicken or pig is sacrificed by the shaman as an offering to the concerned ancestor or spirit. After cooking and eating, the remains are left for the tiger. Apart from the sacrificial act, the occasion involves no other rituals. Issues such as the equitable participation by women in ceremonies are unknown. Words like 'participation' and 'access' come from vocabularies of power and inequality.

Women and men are integral to a natural arrangement and do not flourish when the arrangement ceases to exist. When life is simple and bare, conflicts and issues become superfluous. The social, political, ethical or religious cannot address the issues of the human. Staying amongst trees, animals, insects, soil, space and sky, she and he remain gentle and generous human beings.

8

Burunga the Blacksmith

Burunga the blacksmith lived at the edge of the village. In fact, all seven families of Garpa lived at its edges. At the centre lived the sixty-odd cows and bulls under the open sky. Surrounding the centre were the seven scattered huts; each separated from the other by about a furlong or two. The cows and bulls were village cattle, neither owned nor otherwise. Their days were spent grazing in the jungle and nights in the village. In the village, they sat huddled in a circle; in the middle slept the calves. That was their fortification against the tiger or leopard. When came morning, the cattle left for the jungle to graze just as humans went to gather food. By evening, all returned to their places. People did not milk the cattle; they did not know how to. Milk was not in their diet.

With extensive deposits of high-grade iron ore, Bastar has a long tradition of iron smelting and forging. There is a whole community of blacksmiths. They are called '*gadhwa lohars*' (smelter-blacksmiths). The word comes from Chhattisgarhi and Hindi. They made ploughs, hoes, nails, pots, pans and cowbells. Being situated in Bastar, Abujhmad too has iron deposits but not the tradition of smelting or blacksmithing. Nor does it have a word for the blacksmith. Nevertheless, it has borrowed the nomenclature of 'lohar'. So Burunga was known as 'Burunga the lohar'.

Burunga was the village blacksmith. He was the blacksmith for not only Garpa but for several surrounding villages, of which Garpa was the largest. Everyone knew Burunga as the blacksmith, but blacksmithing he never did; he did not have even the remotest connection to blacksmithing nor was blacksmithing needed in the region. During my five years in Garpa, I never heard or saw Burunga deliver a word or deed that could ascribe to him a business with iron. He did not even have a hammer, anvil, tong or furnace nor did he display any other elementary signs of the trade. In fact, he did not know of them. The axes, arrows and knives of Abujhmadias required only periodic sharpening and shining. That was done by the owners against a piece of rock. Except the axes, arrows and knives—which were acquired from Madai (an annual fair-festival) at Narayanpur, once every two or three years—people did not own any metal.

Blacksmithing had not reached Garpa or Abujhmad. But Burunga was the 'blacksmith' by title and due praise. Why that was so or how he got the rank, or why he was 'needed' I do not know. Nor did I ask. Some questions, most questions, ought not be asked. They do not make sense. The Abujhmadias themselves do not ask questions. About the only association Burunga had with iron was that whereas others in the village were of a soft temperament, he appeared hard and aloof, if not cold too. Not by any means was he one of usual human expressions or gestures. Banda the elder too was like that in thought, speech and behaviour, but when needed, he would rise up and dance, tell a story, crack jokes or sing a song. Burunga did not allow himself such pleasures. He was aloof like the shaman, but shaman he was not.

He went with the other villagers to gather food about twice a week. He was good at sensing or sniffing out animals; rarely did his nose lie. There was something of the goat, dog, cow and tree in his gait and expressions. He could sense and smell better the tiger, leopard, bear or bison, and the group of gatherers would change course or take other measures. He would sit still atop a mound, almost one with it, and stare into dense foliage for long hours for the honeybee headed for the honeycomb. On the days he was not food-gathering, he sharpened his axe, arrowheads and knives, or embellished with rudimentary designs their wooden handles in the fire. Or just sat doing nothing, or wove a tele from bamboo for trapping fish, scooped out a gourd for storing mahua, ground *pogha* (wild tobacco) and animal bone for the family's chewing, made pouches from a tree root to keep the pogha in, or smoothened out bear claws on a rock to put around his daughters' necks. He had a wife and two daughters. Of approximately three and five years, both were sparkling little girls. Like children anywhere in the world, they were high spirited. Much of their time went into playing, running around and laughing, and were often teasingly at loggerheads with me.

Burunga would press me to change the thatch of my roof (an operation undertaken every two or three years, lasting over a week or more each time) lest there be leakage when came the rains. Sure enough, he would not go beyond pressing the advice. Juru, Suku and the others helped me with collecting and changing the thatch. Burunga would also upbraid me for my ignorance in effectively wielding the axe or bow and arrow, but he would not teach me the correct way. Though aloof and distant, he was, however, at much personal risk, the first amongst those who stuffed dry tobacco leaves into the opening in my hut floor through which one day, after a 'whoosh' dreaded as much as a tiger's roar, a cobra had slithered in. He could have been bitten and would have died within twenty minutes. The tobacco leaves were then fired to smoke the snake out through some other opening into the surrounding forest. Burunga felt odd about the tablets for headache, an ailment I have had since childhood, that I carried on me. He could not believe little pills could cure a paralysing headache. He was not too worried about illness and death and did not store any curative herbs or roots. None in the village did, even though he, like everyone else, and his hut, like all huts, were devoid of 'well-being and safety'.

From the distance of his hut, 'Burunga the blacksmith' would keep looking at my door but would almost never talk. He was a good neighbour. Like his two little daughters he was a fine person and fine parent, a nice human being who did not wish to be more than he was. A true son of his wilds, he remained how he was.

9

I Sat By

WHENEVER I could, I sat by. Mostly I could. There seemed no other way. On the other bank of the Kuari sat, like meditative ascetics, the silhouetted and labyrinthine ravines of Chambal Valley. Beyond was the small village of dusty slate roofs, dusty men, women, children, houses, dogs, cattle and trees. Locomotion and behaviours of the village were as stationary as its sky. On the other side of Kuari lived the mango trees, too. There was not much to be or do in those empty ravines. So, like the village, I too sat by.

Legend has it that Kuari, a young maiden, could make the waters of the well rise for her two bullocks to drink. Once when she was praying and the water was rising, someone saw her without clothes. She jumped into the well and died. The well then overflowed and became a river. That is how came the river Kuari.

The rock sat quietly in the flowing waters. Like most little children do, it sat in the middle. Like leaves floating on a gentle wind, the muddy waters of a ripple come dancing and touch the rock. That is when sound is born. Here, it is about the only sound one can hear. Otherwise, there remains the placid flow of waters, winds and lives. Birds sat on the trees and pecked at the mangoes—pecking at one, jumping to the next, savouring each. Like children they do not eat the full mango. Mango to mango, flavour to flavour, tree to tree, shade to shade they flit. Sitting here and there all the way. Birds do not know the way; they are the wayward. Theirs is the way. Theirs is the full that needs less. There always is the full that needs less. Scarcity dwells in stir, toil and pursuit. Birds are not in pursuit, their full remains full. Time ceases when lived idly and unchanged. It cannot then measure locomotion and behaviours—quintessential attributes of stir, toil and pursuit. Stir, toil and pursuit make Space and Time germane to living. In sitting they die. There always remains the full in the small village of dusty slate roofs by the Kuari.

The sun is dipping into the mango trees. Dipping ever since it began coming. So would dip the birds. And the mangoes. And their trees and the village. And the waters. And the dusty slates and sky. All would ultimately die in the dark. The dark would die too. When no one is witnessing, things die. No one sees in the dark. When one does not see, one dies. One who does not see oneself even over a lifetime is dead and unsafe for the earth. Beware.

I do not remember the great author Premchand ever speaking of his characters or their circumstances darkly or despairingly in his voluminous works. Despite their poverty, he ascribes to them ways that enhance them, their circumstance and the reader. Most modern philosophers and authors write with eloquence of darkness and despair. Schopenhauer called the world a penitentiary. Beware.

I tell myself, stop asking. Stop at the very first question. After that it will be difficult. Life will acquire locomotion. One who cannot stop at the first, cannot stop at the next. But if you are already in locomotion and cannot turn back, do not despair. Things will take their inescapable course. Be their instrument, even though they be evil. Allow them their course to annihilate you. One needs dissolution, not evolution. Questions come from estrangement and despair. They come from the un-self that pre-empts one. They have an agenda to fetch that which ought not be fetched. I tell myself to be with myself and there will come no questions. I tell myself to not place confidence in questions. Stop at the very first.

It is evening and darkness is coming out of its own lights. Soon they too will be out with guns, powder and resolute intent. And the moustaches below the fiery eyes, flaring nostrils and stirred hearts that tear apart the small sound of the muddy ripple in the Kuari. Scores have to be settled. Life itself has to be settled since conception and birth. But, ironically, right up to the end it remains unsettled. With or without gun and powder such is the fate of intent and stirred hearts. Scores are continually being settled, mostly with oneself. The very first step annihilates. Beware.

The previous evening, near where I now live in Ghaziabad walked the old bull of stolid hump. Hump swayed from side to side. Of lacerated and dragging hind hoof, he walked straight sans hobble or pain. He alone is without the step, question and locomotion; and alone has the blind eye that does not see the something and the countless. On the narrow trail of dust and droppings, I step aside to give the venerable the rite of passage. He walks by in silence, peace and poise like the waters of Kuari. With folded hands, I bow my head in silent respect. One may not see a sage again.

10
They Were Seiks

For those deprived of landscapes, it is difficult to fathom how people of different faiths and persuasions live together on land. The quarrels and concord, and allowing for differences in everyday living, are not spoken of in the educated and dominant narrative. The same narrative also defines what land, landscape, wilds and village are. Hence, many times it becomes difficult to speak of either. Even when one does, it is considered anecdotal and without worth or value. As an instance, during the subcontinent's partition in 1947, there was no riot of note in all of west Uttar Pradesh despite a large and robust Muslim population residing in the region. Those who migrated did not leave out of religious differences or persecution. They were of the landed peasantry and, with the coming of agrarian land reform that favoured cultivators, saw no future for the zamindari system in post-Independence India. By 1947,[3] it was known that the zamindari system was to be abolished by 1950. For them, migration was more an economic than a religious or political necessity. On the other hand, small or medium cultivators did not leave. They continue to live in the region's villages to this day.

In the villages of west Uttar Pradesh Muslims were known as *Seiks* (Sheikhs) and Hindus as Arya Samajis. In Chhattisgarh, Muslims are referred to as Pathans and other generic nomenclatures elsewhere.

I had not heard of Pakistan till I was twelve years old, or maybe older. When I heard, I did not know what it implied. I found 'Muslim' means something much different from our 'Seik'. Our Seiks were very fine people; and nothing can revise my experience and opinion of them. Even seventy years later, some of their faces remain etched in my mind. When we moved to the city, the maps of India and Pakistan in our schoolbooks introduced us to new concerns and issues that were not ours in the village. Our elders did not read books or newspapers.

Caste names were used commonly by both us Arya Samaji Hindus and the Seiks. Just as there were Arya Samaji Jats, Rajputs, traders and weavers, it was so amongst Seiks too. The refrain among the Seiks was, 'We have changed our religion, not caste, dialect or culture.' We ate the same foods, wore the same clothes and tied our turbans the same way and of the same colour. Seik women wore saris and also salwar kameez. Salwars were both loose and tight at different places owing to what would now be called bad tailoring. The Muslim *tehmand* (a full-length wrap around the legs) had begun to be worn by

---

[3] In Uttar Pradesh, it culminated in the Zamindari Abolition and Land Reforms Act 1950.

Hindu men also, but it was discouraged for 'daughters and daughters-in-law too live in the village'. Unlike the Hindu *dhoti* (a wrap wound between the legs), the tehmand could fly upwards in the winds exposing a man's legs from bottom to the top. So both Seiks and Hindus mostly wore pyjamas. The Arya Samaji Hindu ritual of suspending a deceased person's cot upside down on the wall on the thirteenth day of the person's death (when, it is believed, the deceased finally leaves for their otherworldly abode) was common amongst Seiks too. During a *nikah* (wedding contract between bride and groom), the *qazi* (Muslim priest) would perform Islamic rituals but a *pandit* (Hindu priest) was invited as a formal witness and to bless the couple. Caste and *gotras* (ancestral lineage) were observed by everyone and hence marrying cousins was considered forbidden amongst Seiks too. Except in the very beginning, some few hundred years ago, Seiks never expressed a desire to return to the Arya Samaj fold, nor were the latter willing to accept them back. The case of Rangadhs is interesting here. Folklore has it that when the Hindu soldiers returned to the villages after being held captive in wars with the Afghans, Mongols, Turks, Persians, Mughals and others, they were declined entry into the Arya Samaj fold. As prisoners, they had had to eat the food cooked by their captors, so they had become malech. Many protested that they could not have taken their mothers, wives or sisters to cook for them, and that they should hence be allowed back into the fold. Eventually, they became Seiks but also continued to be Rajputs, Jats and others in habit, behaviour and practice. They began to be called 'Rangadhs' (changed or moulded by war; *ran* = war, *gadh* = mould, cast). They are still called so. The knowledgeable Bhaat would have precise information on our ancestry and significant events that took place in the lineage anywhere from the preceding generation to 1,500 years ago or maybe more. We could find out where a certain ancestor lived or migrated from, his or her name, birth and death, the land he cultivated and the crops he grew, including their quantity in a certain year, whom he married and who his children were. We could also find out when our neighbours became Seiks and under what circumstances. Seiks too followed the Bhaat system. But then, except for finding out their gotras, people were not keen on knowing ancestry or history. Except occasionally, the Bhaat—like the Brahmin—remained of little importance.

They were Seiks, we were Arya Samajis. Just as Islam was un-pronouncedly practised amongst the Seiks, so was Hinduism amongst us. There was a certain earthy ambiguity in both. But we knew of our separateness, too. There was much of the raw country wit around both the religions. They were not a big issue between us as but they became big when the village opened up to the outside world and our knowledge base increased. We need not have known so much; never earlier did. Our common village or regional ancestors and legends began to be replaced by the Buddha, Shankaracharya, Emperor Ashok, Akbar, Vivekanand, Jinnah and the rest; and our folklore by the scriptures.

Sometimes, we ran the Seiks down good-humouredly about their mosques, Mecca, Medina and their aluminium utensils; just as we were not pronouncedly reverential of our own Banaras or Haridwar. The Seiks, too, joked about our temple (the temple always remained unused and unkempt; what it was for I could never know) and the *choti* (tuft of hair) on our Hindu heads. There was one mosque in the village, but to this day I do not know where it was located; it never issued the azaan, just as the temple never a *bhajan* (Hindu hymn). During hot afternoons, after grazing, the cattle went inside the temple for shade and water (there was a pond next to it). Till the Meenakshipuram conversions (1981), our temple lay abandoned and in disuse. Our thoughts and beliefs about ourselves as Arya Samajis were not 'cleansed' by the tenets of scriptural Hinduism or other agencies; there was a certain, as though deliberate, nebulousness and distance from scriptures. This left open many possibilities, including not taking formal beliefs and rituals seriously, making use of witticisms, and maintaining a distance from what is now called the 'Hindu identity'. Beliefs and identities remained light, just like life—to be lived with and not to be died or killed for. There were the occasional small quarrels and fights but they got resolved, too.

Hinduism was followed only broadly and loosely. It was uneducated and earthy. As adherents, we were free to find our own ways of being Hindus, as also of everyday religious and social living. There was not a pressing singularity. Such ways were many times mutually contradictory, too—we were free to have our own kind of native Hindu–Muslim relationship and a rather diffused caste system. Perhaps other regions were different; I cannot say much on this for I have not seen and lived in those regions. We knew and identified ourselves in terms of our village and region rather than pan-India Hindus or Muslims.

It is interesting to consider why the region persistently refused to see its Hinduism, Islam or history in a certain way, until seeing themselves in that extraneous way could be avoided no more. Seeds of the extraneous were sowed not only by the British but also by those revered as torchbearers of scriptural Hinduism, social reformers, political leaders and the rest. The Seik was as distanced from his religious or socio-political heroes as the Arya Samaji from his. Practically none of the torchbearers, social reformers, political leaders and the rest spoke of ordinary people, ordinary ways or ordinary concerns. Kabir and Gandhi were woven into our conversations only feebly; we had little to do with them.

It may well be argued—as it has been a few times—that I am talking of a past, that it is nostalgia at work. But I am talking of no earlier than forty to fifty years ago. It is within touching distance of our memories and many amongst us are still surviving witnesses of that time. Also, 'present', 'past' and 'nostalgia' are categories of the contemporary sensibility, specifically that of the social sciences. They divide the mind and its bearers. Else, the past and the contemporary live together in continuities. They intermingle in the same ways as did we and the Seiks. How easy it is for our ways to be usurped by the artificial framework of naive realism.

We were steadfast Arya Samajis. I do not wish to know how over a mere forty or fifty years our way of Hinduism faded away and we increasingly inclined towards scriptural and educated Hinduism. Nor do I wish to know how in the same period the Seik became a Muslim of the Quran and Sharia. Now, we are different people, no longer the same.

11

Conversations on the Way

A question ought be fundamental and decisive. Else it should not be asked. Only that be asked that puts life at stake. Less makes it trivial.

———•———

There are shadows not only in daylight but also in the primordial dark; shadows without their objects. One needs the ancient dark to see. Eyes see best in the dark.

———•———

A tradition that can converse with its opposite, modernity, tells of how the two are flip sides of the same coin; like people living under the same roof but claiming to be separate.

Hence, the logjam in knowledge systems. The Abujhmadia stands on an altogether different plane. His sheer inconversability is the answer, were one to be sought. When you think you know Abujhmad, it slips away. It is far too shy to converse.

When someone accords with us, we feel that much more accompanied.

Living is an extremely private experience, almost incommunicable. It is about an anonymity within oneself that even the bearer may never know.

It is impossible to know beforehand what to understand, and what not to. Yet, understanding happens on its own. Humans hardly have a role. Like much else, good and otherwise, my experience of Abujhmad happened on its own. That it continues to stay within is also on its own. I have no exertions that I could call mine.

The part is bigger than the whole. Yet, the whole does not break apart. Break apart into what? If the inside is smaller, the outside would collapse. It confuses. Some say I am not pragmatic.

Repugnance and fear, that is how Abujhmadias will respond to excessive organization when they confront it sooner or later.

How to write? May be there is no way. Perhaps it happens on its own. I do not know. But I know it demands forfeiture—of one's own self. More than oneself, it has no other demand.

Outsiders who invaded India were never driven out. Those who went back, did so largely of their own accord once they had their booty and loot. Suppose the British had stayed on like the many others. The movement for Independence was not initiated by the oil presser, potter, carpenter, farmer, weaver or stealer of cattle but by a powerful and enlightened elite. The British were not turned back by native ethos and ways of living but by the elite, who brought 'mass consciousness' to one idea, one that was not our own. Noble and admirable as Gandhi ji is, I have sometimes wondered what if, instead of removing the British, he had stressed only on strengthening the countryside and its ways.

A fact is merely a fact. Only itself. But truth needs both itself and untruth. That is aesthetics. Poet Nirala did not stick to only facts. He spoke both truth and untruth. So did the elders in my childhood village. In between lay the play people lived by. Could there be any greater truth?

And as came the muezzin's call for evening prayers so did the dogs in the fields stop playing and begin to wail. They go to the nearby Hindu temple to enjoy the leftovers of *prasad* (offerings to the gods). Theirs is not an inclination to Hinduism, Islam, Creator or Creation. They are happy to play. In their simple ways, they are infinitely more emulate-able than the believer. Animal and sage are alike.

———◆———

Thoughts are disguised sediments of somewhere. They are unsettled sediments. Beware. Welcome them at your own peril. Or be unsettled yourself.

———◆———

Over the years, some have said I live life on the edge. Though I do not know exactly what it means, I suppose there must be other places too where one might live. But I do not know of them.

———◆———

How could I do something about my life when I myself was carried into it; when I myself have been so unperformed? I am yet to take birth. A naive realism is the new bane of our times.

———◆———

In the early 1960s when I was very young, tea companies used to go door to door distributing tea leaves free of cost during the winters. With better fare to eat and drink, people did not like tea. But after some time, and with persistent persuasion and lures of which only companies and merchants know, we began drinking tea because it came free. Teatime was also leisure time, in fact, much of those were leisure times. Everyone began drinking tea, several times a day and in all seasons. Now there is neither that milk, that tea nor that leisure, those seasons, that health or well-being. Merchants took the seasons and well-being away.

As I write I die, too, in the same measure.

A few days ago, an eminent journalist of an equally eminent online daily said that the ordinary people of India will soon wake up and do the needful. Of the two, who is asleep?

Lokman Dikshit, popularly known as Lukka, was a legendary *baghi* (rebel) of the Chambal ravines. The British called the baghis 'dacoits'. The word persists to this day. Lukka was of one of the highest moral statures in the thousands of villages in the Chambal region spread over three states. The region had its own holy men, bards, leaders and eminent citizens. Lukka was from the Maan Singh band. He was fondly called Raja Maan Singh by the people and police. After Maan Singh was killed by deceit, the band—now led by Lukka—surrendered to Vinoba Bhave in 1960. Surrender took place in one of Vinoba's daily prayer meetings during the Bhoodan Yatra (Land Donation Movement). Lukka or the band did not know of Vinoba or his stature and had barely heard of Gandhi ji. They looked upon him as some good-hearted saint who was seeking land for the poor in the villages. There they were, the erudite ascetic and the illiterate baghi, an ex-farmer. The two saw each other in the dim light of a lantern during an evening prayer meeting and melted. Thus in 1960 began the 'Dacoit Surrender', the first in more than 800 years of baghi lineage in the Chambal ravines. Lukka was every inch an emperor; such was his demeanour when I first saw him in dhoti–kurta one day in 1977 amidst the earthen mounds of Modhana Jawahar village. So was Banda the Abujhmadia in 1980. In his bare body and a loin cloth, he was every inch an emperor and as majestic as Lukka. In word and demeanour both were economists of a high order. Except that Vinoba was more talkative, there was little to distinguish between Vinoba, Lukka and Banda.

———•———

There is little or nothing in contemporary times that tells, 'It is alright to be who and where you are.' We suffer from an implanted deficiency syndrome.

———•———

The coming, without footfalls, of shame and ignominy.

———•———

How could there be unless there be? It was scarcely disguised.

———•———

Silence is there—like the sun, winds and moon. It does not come from something; it is neither created, nor acquired. You cannot sail into silence as it were. One must put aside all that one has known and valued and step into that that is too mundane to be called known. Knowing does not mean anything, nor non-knowing; neither is there a knower or a known. It is about living without knowing what happened.

It is not advancement or augmentation that will sail me into it but complete abatement and disintegration.

Usually, the shaman cast a spell if his sister or daughter's love remained unreciprocated by a boy. Though there were shamans, there were not witches.

Mother used to say, 'You do not like human company.' It was not merely a matter of liking or disliking. I felt insecure and fearful in human company; at times stuttering or tremulous. Even as a child, I was good at hiding. Seventy years later I have not changed much; neither have humans nor situations.

There are the well-timed and the ill-timed, the right time and wrong time. But, in effect, there is neither. Wherever I am is the beginning and the closure.

Language is of assumptions. Dialect is about a perpetual rawness and newness of earth. For dialect, life is a continual novelty. Language is tired and despairing, it articulates. Dialect conceals–reveals.

———•———

I do not remember ever hearing a folk song of despair in Bastar or my childhood village.

———•———

One's given station in life is more affectionate and protective than one knows.

———•———

Silence is the emptiness and veeran without a background or foreground. It does not change; nor is it changeless. It remains and remains-not, no matter how many voices and voicelessnesses come and go.

———•———

Abujhmad is like an infant who considers its body a toy. Like the infant, it needs neither religion nor history or geography to play with.

———•———

Anxieties to save the world, times or money stem from insecure, guilt-ridden and agitated souls. Beware.

———•———

For several years, I have not seen a sparrow and its dust bath.

———•———

Someone brought the news he is dead. But when did he live? He died dead.

———•———

Reaching was not its aspiration; it was no one's. The urge to reach stemmed from stir and agitation. The issue is not reaching or not reaching; it is stir and agitation. Only when in stir and agitation does one wish to move, change or seek.

———•———

That trail was empty of purpose or function, devoid of seeking or reaching. Traveller and trail became one.

———•———

Seeking, attachment and commitment determine the landscape, social or natural. So does their absence. Truth happens in abeyance. All trails are to abeyance.

———•———

Stop giving energies to doing or seeking. Instead, energies ought go into giving up to the landscape, for then there are needed neither doing nor seeking, neither giving up nor overcoming; neither self nor non-self. Activity, initiative, energetic willingness and robust self-assertion are means to conjuring up the doer.

Seekers and doers are antithetical to the landscape. As against the effortless, a vigorous will and assertion of the self are then needed for everyday living. Eventually, it becomes perpetually being who one did not wish to be.

There came fear. It came because falsehood begets fear. How much materiality do I need to live a simple, healthy and happy life? Similarly, how much knowledge, or even virtue, do I need to live a simple, healthy and happy life? How much consideration do I need to give to anything in any case? There is the loss of vitality to be.

I have seen it time and again. I have also seen that passivity and idleness are honourable virtues amongst people with landscapes. I have seen inertness and idleness happening over the years in not only the inanimate but also the animate. They are the premises on which they live. Anything else is futile and false.

12

Tiger in the Twilight

'An infallible method of conciliating a tiger is to allow oneself to be devoured.'

—Konrad Adenauer

THAT morning had been stormy. The sky, however, had cleared up soon after. Dark clouds had gone away to wherever they lived. It was again the clear blue sky of stationary white clouds. The ground, though, had turned watery and slippery. One had to be firm footed on the trail, especially on descents. Then, walking barefoot is the best for toes to dig in better into the slippery earth. It was only in situations like these that I could do away with my rubber slippers. Many a tree had fallen and large boulders rolled off their holds. The forest, nevertheless, had turned a smiling green. Monsoon is the time of grandeur in the wilds. It is also the time when apart from animals, snakes and insects come out and roam freely. Black scorpions larger than a human palm, and of fatal stings, are to be particularly watched out for.

We were returning from the village of Kohkameta. Having left it a little over two hours earlier, we were nearing Garpa, the village of my residence. It was around twilight. The sky was sending down its first dark shadows like apparitions. Things had gradually begun changing into silhouettes. A ritual of evenings, they always did that. First, they blur, then dimly silhouette and eventually dissolve into the formless dark, without even a vestige left behind. Peculiar to nights here, that dark stillness— felt in one's bones— had begun emerging slowly and ominously. We were on the last incline. Another twenty or so minutes away lay the small plateau whereupon sat the seven huts of Garpa. Unlike the nights of the full moon, when the jungle is papered with silver, this was a moonless night.

I was with Professor Suresh Sharma from Delhi. A philosopher, historian and cultural anthropologist, he had come visiting Abujhmad for his research work. I was a part of the work till opting out six months after coming here. There is much that I have learnt from Professor Sharma and owe him a lot. He was a close and deeply respected friend, philosopher and guide.

Suresh was a rather slow walker, which in this instance was also partly because of the terrain. Here, it sometimes worried me. He certainly seemed to like it. Nevertheless, approaching darkness persuaded him to increase his pace. We were talking with each other a little more loudly than we did at other times of the day. Talking was as much to reassure ourselves as to keep the animals at bay. In the jungle, it is good to let animals know that humans too are on the trail. That can prevent the sudden encounters (unless it is a bear) that may sometimes turn fatal for humans.

The trail straightens out somewhat just before Garpa. Tired, looking down and talking, we walked one behind the other, occasionally looking up to see that all was well. As we looked up once again, there appeared the most dreaded sight in the jungle. It was a tiger. Apparently, it had not gone away even when it heard us talk. Instead, barely twenty yards away, it sat right in the middle of the trail. We could faintly see its yellow in the dwindling light. Sitting on hindquarters like a dog (usually tigers sit on all fours or lie down in the manner of sleeping), it was looking in our direction. Our steps froze and throats dried up. Talking ceased abruptly. For the outside world, a tiger is an animal. In the wilds, the substance of a tiger is the very elemental darkness that dismantles and devours all—forms, bodies and lives. As nights come, people huddle into tiny huts and burn fires to dispel both tiger and the elemental dark.

Without sensation or thought, we stood benumbed in body and mind; not a finger stirred. To say that body and mind had turned blank would be an understatement. Such is the unfamiliarity of some moments that they may not be described. However, so frozen and wooden were we that we no longer knew there were two of us. People say one ought to stand frozen when in the presence of a tiger, not a limb or eyeball should move. 'Be stock-still.' That now happened effortlessly. People also say, when face to face with a human, the tiger almost invariably walks away. Before that, however, it appraises one's intent. The human is on trial. 'Is it really a chance meeting or is it otherwise?' Those few moments of furious and deep growls are sounds of the netherworld. Going down on the forelegs and twirling its tail, the tiger scratches the ground with its paws so powerful that they can shatter a human skull as can a human an egg. So benumbed is one that 'it does not hurt when one is mauled and killed'. Death is mercifully painless.

That it was rapidly turning dark now was not a good note. We stood looking at the animal motionlessly, it at us. A hushed twenty yards lay in between—about a mid-sized leap for a tiger. It can leap upon the victim thirty yards away in a fraction of a second. From where we were, there was no other way to Garpa. Had we tried one, we would have lost our way and wandered the night in the yet deeper wilds. It is easy to lose one's sense of direction here, more so at night. Going back to Kohkameta was not possible, either. We would have met other animals. Also, turning back makes it suspicious and can be fatal. Neither was the animal going away nor letting us go. Twenty minutes passed like this. Not a growl came or tail twirled. Usually whatever happens, either way, is over in five or six minutes. In the meantime, however, some normalcy and sensation was being restored to our minds and bodies.

Having waited a 'long time' and since the stalemate continued, axe firmly in grip, I took half a step backwards. In Abujhmad, everyone carried an axe. Of multiple uses, it is akin to carrying a *lathi* (baton), a practice in many parts of the country. Though I too carried an axe, I did not know how to use it. Nevertheless, it added to my confidence. An axe is not a weapon, just as a lathi is not. As a weapon, a lathi might be used only once or twice in a lifetime—in most cases not even once. There are no weapons in the wilds. The bow and arrow are for hunting and the axe for cutting, repairing or hammering; or for making way through dense vegetation when looking for cattle killed by a tiger or leopard off the trail.

Though not much used, it is carried practically everywhere. Using one effectively, however, cannot be learnt unless one grows up amidst them. Their texture, tensity and usage then sink in and the axe becomes a companion if not an external limb. Even when the Abujhmadia is jumping across a stream, climbing a tree or running down a hill face, the axe blade remains perched firmly on his shoulder.

Even as I stepped back in the continued stalemate, the tiger's gaze in our direction remained unchanged. In the dark, whereas human sight is compromised, tigers retain excellent vision. That movement of even half a step should have invited a leap instantly. But nothing happened. That was odd behaviour. A little later, I took a step forward. Suresh did likewise. This time, too, nothing happened. For the first time, I wondered what animal it really was. That gave us a little heart and comfort; little but much in those moments. Groping for a pebble with my toes, I picked one and softly cast it in its direction. There was still no leap or growl. In the stillness, there had not been any wind to carry over to us the foul odour that tigers emit. The odour tells one how far the animal is and in which direction. Despite the deepening dark and no odour, the tiger's contours were still visible. Haltingly, we took another tiny step forward, and then another. Terror still in our hearts, we were nearing it but there was also some hope now. With about ten yards left, Suresh beamed his powerful torch in its direction. It took us a while to register that it was a dead and broken stump of a tree. In the morning, when we had passed that way, it had not been there. The stump must have rolled down in the storm from a nearby mound and come to rest on the trail. Its rest was such that the contours resembled a tiger sitting on its haunches. The stump had been washed clean in the heavy rain and had become of a lighter colour. Standing beside it, reassuring ourselves, we hesitantly felt it with frozen fingers.

Losing no time in thanking our stars, and because danger could still be lurking nearby, we resumed our walk. Throats continued to be parched. Upon entering the hut and lighting the fire we spoke again, but not about the tiger that deceived. We never did.

13

Of Parvati's Wedding

A simpleton's enduring quality is that he has only small fights with himself and others. In one way or another, my urban-educated generation has been habitually querulous and complaining. Quarrel, complain and change the times were considered a pre-requisite to progressive living. They were important drivers of much of one's political and personal activity. Nurtured in the consciousness of social and other sciences instead of a landscape's, my generation also considered itself to be of erudition and muscle to fundamentally change the simpleton's inherited discourse and way of looking at himself and life. While disapproving of him and his ways, we wished to change the premise his life stood on. Where he stood, however, was neither the querulous nor the complaining, neither the demanding nor the giving. We of our generation came from various, and opposing, political persuasions and indoctrinations.

We were quarrelling with the State, capitalist, communist, tradition, inertia, restfulness, natural rhythms of life and were also at conflict amongst and within ourselves. Of a discontented egalitarianism, angry feminism, family and relationships, we were re-interpreting the past and engineering an unseen future in nearly complete disagreement with the simpleton. Intolerant almost to the extreme in our reappraisals of his or her heroes, legends and symbolisms like Ram and Sita, fairs and festivals, rituals and practices, which were thrown to the sidelines, he was made to feel foolish and small. In his ignorance, inertia and restfulness, he could dilute and stitch together identities as Hindu and Muslim, adivasi and non-adivasi, peasant and landlord, creating a fusion that the social sciences could neither grasp nor make sense of.

Paradoxically, in order that justice, peace and love come to prevail eventually, we needed an enemy and hatred to live by. For that, we devised a suitable vocabulary. It was used, promoted and well-regarded by our mutually inimical orientations and indoctrinations. It was all in the name of the simpleton. But also, and again ironically, it was a vocabulary the simpleton had neither heard of nor could understand. The same vocabulary was equally well regarded and promoted by the State. We and the State had the same conceptions of the world and its things while mock fighting each other. The fight was also in the name of justice, peace, love and the simpleton. It was a blindness that comes from forgotten self-appraisal.

The idea of an external enemy was seductive. There being little or nothing of the landscape in us, had someone like Gandhi ji taken away the enemy, my generation would have collapsed; but Gandhi ji was killed. Whether adivasi, Dalit, woman or peasant, all ideas and movements were, and are, based on belligerence and vitriol. For us were the progressive and great writers, while the earthy and conciliating Tolstoy and Premchand were on decline. A few decades ago I was at an event at a very premiere and progressive university in Delhi when I received an earful for wasting away in primitive Abujhmad when I should have been elsewhere in solidarity with the progressives. Not only my benefactor's argument, it was also his confidence that had left me witless. He was younger by quite a few years and very well-read for his age but, like, me rooted nowhere.

A minor exception in my generation were the Gandhian Sarvodayans. They had not been much absorbed in the progressive mainstream. They came largely from the landscapes of villages and small towns, and spoke of heroes, legends and symbols like Ram and Sita, fairs and festivals, rituals and beliefs; and still used coconut or mustard oil in the hair. Speaking in their native dialects, they did not think much beyond their own villages and regions. Without the encroachment by the persona created by the social sciences, there was still the indistinct and metaphorical to their ways. In times of global progressivism, Sarvodayans were obviously marginalized as wishy-washy, unread, of weaker intelligence and of unclear ideas.

Once during a train journey when I began reading the Bhagvat Katha, I came across the story of how Himalaya and his spouse Maina married their daughter Parvati with Shiv. Himalaya and Maina had invited to their daughter's wedding the various mountain ranges from across the world along with several heavenly beings and celestial bodies. The account is narrated by Brahma the Creator to His son Narad, the celestial storyteller and sage, also a messenger between the past, present and future. It was a narration whose magnitudes were spellbinding, yet there was to it the flavour as though the wedding was happening in one's own neighbourhood. That conception of an earthly occasion fusing effortlessly into the infinite celestial had left me awed and speechless. That copy of the Bhagvat Katha was eaten away by termites in Bastar and I could never buy another. Also, by that time I had moved more into Abujhmad, the region of the nebulous and indistinct, all revealing and all concealing—a region of veritable hide and seek that children play effortlessly every day. The Bhagvat Katha was gone yet it remained. As time went by in Abujhmad, Bastar and other areas, I began finding an ease in most of the faces I happened to come across, and began suspecting that I faintly knew where their ease came from. The old woman sitting atop her ramshackle push-cart selling beedis, cigarettes and goodies near my house in Ghaziabad; the tea-seller maulana, who dislikes customers; the cobbler by the *nullah* (drain) working ceaselessly with ease; the bulls, goats, cows and the sparse fields near where I now live; or Astu and Banda of Bastar; or the face of my village of childhood. Theirs is the ease that I think of when remembering the Creator's narration of Parvati's marriage.

In the same vein, I remember Krishnanand ji. Krishnanand ji was an ascetic who roamed Chhattisgarh's villages, reciting the Ramayan every night. There were many others who roamed like he did. Krishnanand ji had a small band of followers; sometimes also called the Gammat Party. 'Gammat' in Chattisgarhi means dance, frolic and learning. Year after year, cold or hot, Krishnanand ji and his band narrated the Ramayan (which people knew by heart in any case) for around three or four nights in a village and then moved to the next. Very often, when the band moved to the next village, many from the previous would visit there at night, listen to the narration and return to their village the next morning. This pattern was repeated over the following nights. Thus had come a chain of continuities. Even though they did not bring any economic or other worldly benefits—nor spoke of inequality, exploitation, injustice and the rest—people like Krishnanand ji were much revered and listened to. People offered food and shelter; and many a time clothing. Often, they were requested to extend their stay in a place. One night, after attending the narration of an episode from the Ramayan, I privately requested Krishnanand ji to tell me more about Ram. He asked me which Ram I wished to hear of. A little astonished, I said that I wanted to know more about the Ram of Ramayan. To that he replied there are several Rams in Ramayan; which one did I wish to know of. I insisted half-heartedly that there is only one Ram. Krishnanand ji replied there are many—Ram the God, king, son, brother, husband, father, friend, warrior, ascetic, disciple, passenger in the *kevat's* (boatman's) boat, the exile in Dandakaranya, and more. In each form, he was complete. Which of his forms did I wish to know of? Each of his forms is a Ramayan. Though always close to my heart and imagination since childhood, I could have never known of Ram in that way. I came away from Krishnanand ji low in spirits at my own ignorance. Later, however, I met him several times elsewhere.

Some decades have gone by. To this day, I remain unable to figure out where to place in our countryside the enemy, vitriol and indoctrination.

14

Chandan bhai

Each village had its own Chandan bhai. The narrow and potholed road from Morena terminated at village Baghchini. From Baghchini ran a dirt track of about five to seven kilometres to village Modhana Jawahar. Modhana sat by the river Kuari in the ravines of Chambal Valley. On the other bank of Kuari stood the mango trees I have spoken of earlier.

Old and toothless Chandan bhai lived in Modhana. He must have been about sixty-five years old. Not even so much as a goat or cow he had, neither a house; nor did he seem to wish for them. Where he lived in the village I did not know and never tried to find out. But he stayed somewhere. I stayed a little outside the village. Wanderer, homeless and penniless, such ways were not unknown in our villages of old mores and doings. That he was from the region was evident from his dialect and mannerisms. Years ago, he had come from his native place and happened to find station here. Where he originally belonged to I did not know. Some details ought not be known about some people; knowings are often needless and irrelevant. Clad in a wrinkled and carelessly tied dhoti, and a borrowed kurta either too large or small, he felt himself a man of good luck. Darkness that may have befallen him some time, he gave no impression of. Chandan bhai was full of mirth and light-heartedness.

He had already been in Modhana for several years when I reached there. I happened to live there for about a year and a half during the course of the baghi surrenders conducted by Gandhians in the second half of 1970s.

Of hollow cheeks and spirited eyes, Chandan bhai received food, clothing and shelter from buffoonery and what are considered frivolities in a world inspired by other attentions. Living was his bidding and he mimicked it well. Never shying away from jokes about himself, he laughed zestfully when others, especially youngsters, laughed at him or his antics. Often, he was the butt of jokes. Of ascetic ways, he certainly was not one; but he was carefree and self-denying. Mimicking life as it had come to him was a service he rendered to the village, such as is most needed and nurtured by healthy societies. People laughed, yet considered him with a degree of seriousness. He was cared and provided for. I do not remember his disaffection or hear him complain about something or someone. That is how he lived. Sometimes he worked as a daily wage earner but preferred not to, for about work he was spiritless. The '*Laanguriya*' (a devotional folk song for Kaila Devi, the region's presiding deity) was one hymn he could sing throughout the night in his squeaky, breaking and needlessly high-pitched voice. Even though the song was devotional, people would laugh uproariously but he would not relent. He liked to call himself a 'singer of repute' and derived much satisfaction from it. There was something of the tentative and half-defined to him. Neither was he the toothless old man nor the little boy of antics, neither a man of this world nor otherwise. There remained to him a vulnerability that secured his feet deep into Mother Earth.

When I was out somewhere, he would sneak into my tent in the outskirts of the village. Fastening together the flaps of the tent, he would stealthily smoke a *beedi* or two so that the other villagers would not find out. Little did he realize that everyone knew. Once when I returned early, Chandan bhai was lying in my bedding on the floor, one knee atop the other, and smoking away. Smoking in a tent is inadvisable for reasons of inflammability. Also, working with the Gandhians as I was, smoking, consuming alcohol and non-vegetarian food were taboo. Chandan bhai knew this. Embarrassed upon seeing me, he stubbed out the ungodly *beedi* into the loamy soil, sat up and began sorting the bedding. We did not speak about it. But he continued drawing the flaps whenever I was away for work in the ravines or other villages. Like the *Laanguriya*, the *beedi* too was a weakness for him; else he was a teetotaller. Sometimes he would take an afternoon nap in the tent. Eventually, from wherever he lived in the village, he shifted into my tent one day. His sole earthly goods were the ill-fitting clothes on his frail body. So long as I remained there, he stayed with me. When I went away on work he would not accompany me. As mentioned, work, of any kind, was not his calling. Somehow, I felt he did not consider it worth his salt to be useful or relevant to the times or to himself.

Each morning he would bring me tea in a chipped enamel mug with the affection and care that belong solely to people of rich cultures. Once he picked up the whistle—to be used only in emergencies (which never occurred) vis-à-vis the baghis, which

Chandan bhai knew well—from under my pillow without my knowing. That day as some of us were crossing the Kuari to pluck some mangoes he began blowing it incessantly. The false alarm could have had some unhappy consequences. That day I was a little annoyed. But Chandan bhai did not deserve annoyance from any quarter, though it came sometimes.

I do not think he knew of anything beyond the village and the Kuari. Or knew anything of what an outsider like me knows and leaves practically no stone unturned to know yet more. Turning stones are a knower's tidings. It seemed that even what Chandan bhai knew was not of much worth for him, and he lived accordingly. Chandan bhai was steeped deep. Not only was he completely illiterate and unread, he had, till the coming of baghi surrender, not even heard of Gandhi ji. It was neither relevant nor important. There was hardly anything to learn from him nor did he have to teach. *Sangat* (congress) with such people is sufficient good luck.

Some years later I reached Abujhmad. One day Chandan bhai passed away. He had lived lightly and wisely. He is a reminder of the discreet distances one ought to keep from life and oneself. Much lionizing or intimacy are deemed unwise.

In many ways, each village was a Chandan bhai.

15

Strangers, Friends and Well-Wishers—My Good Samaritans

AMONG the few purposeful travels I have undertaken one was when I went from Delhi to Puducherry. That, if I now remember correctly, was in 1975. I was twenty-one years old. Knowing of no other place, I had gone to Aurobindo Ashram looking for inner peace (a terrible thing to be looking for at twenty-one). I could not have known enough about either life or peace; nor do still. The undertaken purpose aborted a year later. For no fault of the Ashram, my unripened and impatient years were tiring of it. I had a wish to go away but where to, I did not know. There came the wish to walk along the sea to Kanyakumari, the southernmost tip of the subcontinent where over millions of years this ancient land continues to wash itself with the Indian Ocean. After purchasing an umbrella and a pair of tyre slippers, with forty paisa left in the pocket, I started on my way. Kanyakumari was about 500 to 600 kilometres away and was to take about a month to reach.

In a little over an hour I was all alone on the open coast; as though life and its affairs had ended behind in Puducherry. How eloquent open spaces are, how well they accommodate! Soon and unexpectedly, however, the sea and sky began booming and bellowing from some deep-under. The sea began building waves upon waves. There built up the rumble and the roar, the storm, utter darkness and furious gales. Lightning tore apart the sky as it did the sea. It was difficult to walk steady. In spite of the large new umbrella, purchased only hours ago, I was drenched within minutes. Winds were forcing it away while I held tight. Soaked and cold, I looked for shelter. A little ahead, the dim contours of a boat upturned on sand were unmistakable. About twenty feet long, it looked abandoned and decrepit. My stay at Puducherry had been educational in some ways, insofar as I could figure out the inverted boat was abandoned and no longer in use. Lifting a corner of the hull with both hands, I slid under. It was safe there. Wood has its nurturing warmth; just that the boat's bottom which should have been under my feet in other circumstances was now over my head. That is how life and its affairs sometimes turn. With it over my head, albeit leaky, the broken umbrella worked better. But drenched, hungry and alone there was now unhappiness creeping in, too. This is not what I had thought of sea, life or 'pilgrimage' to Kanyakumari.

An hour or two later the storm subsided and it was time to come out from underneath and look for a village for food and better shelter. But the boat would not lift. Having soaked water, its wood was now heavy. Trying as hard as I could, the boat refused to budge. With not a soul in the vicinity I felt trapped for life. Exhausted and distressed, there was, it seemed, nothing left more than giving up and sitting back. Thus, sitting back, however, I began digging out the wet sand. Soon enough I slithered out from underneath the boat. The earth was as battered and drenched by the storm as I was. On its uneven and slippery surface, and without a light, it was not possible to see where the feet were going. The tyre slippers had turned a bad buy; they were slipping more often than holding. Soon they went into the shoulder bag. After another four kilometres some shimmering lights were seen at a distance. It was a village.

As the lights neared, there appeared some villagers chatting under a dim lamp post. The storm had destroyed some houses. Apparently, that had brought them together to discuss it as they stood under the lamp post. Strangely, the lamp post had managed to continue shining. However, approaching a group of men at midnight in an unknown village whose houses stood destroyed was not a good prospect. Seeing a stranger drenched and muddied, village dogs barked and the men looked at me suspiciously. They did not know English or Hindi nor I, Tamil. I could not explain who I was or why I was there. After a few infructuous exchanges, I gestured for food and shelter for the night. But their hostile gestures insisted on knowing who I was and why I was in their village deep into the night. Angry and despairing of the damage to their houses, their aggression was palpable. Several futile questions and gesticulations later, still suspicious and hostile, they began walking me in a certain direction. I did not know where we were headed or what for. That it could not be for shelter and hospitality was reasonably clear. Some men, a few children, several dogs and I formed the small procession through debris and slush. Eventually we stopped at a Mr So-and-So's doorstep. Mr So-and-So worked at a post office in another village and was on a visit to his sister here. Being in the postal department, he knew a smattering of English. Explaining I had set out from Aurobindo Ashram for Kanyakumari and had gotten caught in the storm, I told him I needed food and shelter. He was nice and gentle; that gave me heart. After a few more questions and answers, I washed up and waited while his sister cooked a meal.

A delicious meal of rice, sambar and pickles served on fresh plantain leaf over, Mr So-and-So took me to the village school to sleep. Understandably, he could not have sheltered me in his sister's house. There were many goats, cows, dogs, cats and fleas seeking refuge in the school verandah; the ground outside was too muddy for anyone's comfort. The quadrupeds seemed to disapprove of my sleeping amidst them but more on this some other time. While the creatures and I looked at each other, Mr So-and-So took leave. He did invite me to breakfast the next morning.

At three o'clock, quietly thanking Mr So-and-So and his sister, I again took to walking the seaside for Kanyakumari. It was around eight in the morning when I reached Cuddalore under a blazing sun. After the night's experience and another five hours of walking, the longing for Kanyakumari faded and disappeared altogether. The Ashram seemed good again. But, the thirty or so kilometres that I would have to walk back seemed daunting, certainly so along the sea. Its waters had betrayed the previous night. After a few futile attempts, I met a drugstore owner, who was godsend, gave me the bus fare to Puducherry. After a bath, lunch and a nap, which he thought I needed at his residence located immediately behind the store, I took leave of this kind soul. It was seven in the evening when I was back in Daya bhai's dormitory at the Ashram. The month-long 'pilgrimage' to Kanyakumari was aborted overnight. The tip of this ancient landmass has not been seen by this author to this day.

Strangers, Friends and Well-Wishers—My Good Samaritans

Though there did not come the peace I had naively wished for, spending those months at the Ashram was a touching experience of the essential goodness in humans. Its full worth, confessedly, reached me only a few years later. The Ashram had quite a few guest houses and dormitories. Daya bhai was the manager of the dormitory where I lived. Not only did he allow me to stay free of cost but also had secured excellent Indian and continental meals without cost from the Ashram's central mess for the year. In both cases, he had to go out of his way. The indulgence of a gratis and affectionate mug of coffee and country cheroot each morning by Anna the shack owner came of a love too deep and precious to be told. Anna also treated me to Tamil movies once a week even though I did not understand the language. A complete stranger, he had become my local guardian of sorts; even though we did not understand each other's language. Apart from these two, I knew only a few others.

A year after coming to Puducherry, I left it in 1977. When I reached Vinoba's Paunar Ashram (formally known as Brahm Vidya Mandir) after this, unlike Puducherry, it was not to seek peace. Experience had begun subtly denting naiveté of that kind. The visit was to see—only see—for a day or two, the living saint and associate of Gandhi ji who had spent decades in close companionship with the Mahatma. Somehow, my fondness for Gandhi ji had always been there; and for Vinoba ever since I first saw a pencil sketch of his face in my Hindi schoolbook. Unknown to one, some things tuck away deep in one only to reappear years later when they do. Vinoba had that which draws one to another. *Darshan* (beholding) has a high significance in the Indian mind and culture. Seeing is enough, even without understanding or knowing. Just seeing. I was still inexperienced enough to know that darshans do not 'pay' in life. In hindsight, I am fortunate there was the inexperience. As life gradually unfolds, shortcomings too become blessings.

After alighting from the train at Wardha, there was to be an hour-long bus ride to Paunar. Due to a miscalculation, I got down at the next station, Nagpur. Since there was not the money to pay as penalty for overshooting the journey, I was handed over to the police and detained at the railway police station. The bus fare—which I could not have parted with—was in any case insufficient as a fine. Where I should have been charged under the law and jailed for three months, the police, after some initial harassment, released me a few hours later. This despite the crumpled *lungi* (a wrap around the legs) and unkempt country vest that do not serve as signifiers of good credentials of one thus detained. Eventually, I reached Paunar by the last bus at around ten in the night.

Paunar Ashram was far too ordinary looking. Unlike Aurobindo Ashram, here there was no one around to be seen; as though it were an abandoned place. Running waters of the adjacent Dham river were the only signs of life. The village of Paunar lay across the Dham. While walking towards a silhouetted barrack-like structure of a half-broken asbestos roof, there came briskly two women in my direction. Hearing of my wish to have a darshan of Vinoba, Manju and Sonali said I could see him in the morning, and that for now I should go to the roadside, eat at the tea shack and sleep there or by the river. Till then I had not known the Ashram was only for women ascetics, the only two exceptions being Vinoba himself and Bal bhai, his secretary. With such prospects available, I had to eventually tell of my detention by the police and consequent delay in arriving there; I told them that it was the first time I was in this part of the country and, after the bus fare, I had no money left to eat with.

Strangers, Friends and Well-Wishers—My Good Samaritans

Such is the warmth and goodness of womanhood the world over that not only was I given the barrack to sleep the night but could eventually spend a year at the Ashram.

I was once travelling from Jabalpur to Raipur and then on to Bastar. It was summer. I was cycling down the distance of about 550 kilometres. Evening, and the forlorn stillness it brings, had already arrived. There is a place immediately short of Chilpi *Ghati* (a hilly pass) wherefrom begins a thin, steep and circuitous descent of several kilometres to the other end of the Ghati. It is a densely forested terrain. I had crossed it earlier once or twice by bus. As the descent neared, I saw an elderly couple coming from the opposite direction. Bent, they were carrying on their heads loads of grass and firewood. Signalling me to stop and after the initial greetings were over, they suggested I ought not proceed further, 'Bears and leopards roam the Ghati after dark. There are no villages to seek shelter in and you may come to harm.' They suggested I spend the night with them and resume my journey at dawn. That they were poor and infirm was evident.

At the hut the elderly lady laid out a cot for me to rest on. The elderly man filled up two buckets from the well. After a refreshing bath, while I sat on the cot, the lady kept talking and cooking on the firewood she had just brought. Where had I come from and where was I headed? Why on a bicycle when there are two buses during the day? Where did my parents and siblings live? She was cooking a meal reasonably elaborate for her means. As the conversation went along, I asked, 'Mother, why are you both doing so much for me? I will spend only a night here. You do not know me nor are we likely to meet again.' She paused from blowing into the hearth. 'I have a son your age. He lives far away in the town. Should ever a trouble befall him—as may have upon you this evening—I wish someone would protect him.'

When leaving the next morning, I could not think of a way to thank the elderly couple. There was some money in my pocket but rarely had I felt so poor and insufficient. Bowing and touching their feet, I rode away. I do not know, nor have met, their son, but the kinship continues.

On another occasion, I had gone to Chaampa. It was around eight in the evening when I reached. Chaampa is seventy kilometres from Bilaspur, Chhattisgarh. A small and unhurried town, it had slept off by that time. Those were my early days in Chhattisgarh. I was to eat and sleep at the sole lodge whose name, after forty years, I do not now recollect. It was probably *Chhaya* (shadow) Lodge. Whereas I got a room there, I did not then know that lodges did not provide meals. Eating had to be outside at roadside *dhabas* (eating shacks). The lodge owner informed me that there were three dhabas in the town but they had wound up for the day. I could try my luck, however. I had ridden a good distance across rough country on a borrowed and old-fashioned Rajdoot motorcycle. Rajdoots were elementary and reliable machines. They could be repaired by even a cycle mechanic. A long iron nail could serve as the ignition key were one to lose it and the vehicles were light enough to be dragged should the need arise. No longer in production now, it was the perfect horse for the countryside. Despite being tired, I set out looking for the dhabas. The first two had closed. So had the third. It had 'Marwari Basa' (Marwari's Dhaba) hand-written on it. Hungry and hesitant, I knocked on the door a few times. An elderly man in a rather ruined vest and dhoti, and holding aloft a dim lantern, opened the door. Visibly annoyed, he asked gruffly what brought me to him so late in the night. 'There is no food at this hour. Go away and let us sleep.' I nervously added that I would not mind eating the leftovers from noon or evening, and pay extra for intruding 'so late' in the night; that a simple thaali of *dal-chawal* (plate of lentils and rice) will do. Saying there were no leftovers either he shooed me away and, muttering something, shut the door. Hungry and crestfallen, as I turned towards the motorcycle, the door opened again and he asked me to come in, the gruffness and mutter unchanged. Inside, the dhaba was dim and dark. The lantern was evidently not bright enough. There were many spiderwebs in the thatch ceiling held up by low and greasy logs. An empty gunny bag was spread on the earthen floor to sit on. It had 'Kisan Urea' and the rising sun stencilled in bold blue. The elder placed an earthen lamp in the blackened recess of the mud wall opposite me. There were calendars of gods and goddesses, and famous sages peacefully meditating under some serene fruit-laden trees of Heaven. Alongside were pictures of famous film actors, sportspersons and gents in fashionable hairstyles. Gods, goddesses, sages, actors, sportspersons and hairstyle models, all lived together under one small roof. People are at peace with much in the world. In their invisible ways, they keep it liveable. Sounds of pots, pans, crackling firewood and conversations from another portion of the dhaba offset the gods, goddesses and the rest. Soon came out a sparkling copper thaali of steaming hot and freshly cooked lentils, rice, pickle, freshly cut onions and a fried *papad* (a thin and crunchy accompaniment). Upon eating, as I rose to pay and take leave, the elder declined the payment, the gruff tone still unchanged. On being pressed, he said in his unfriendly way that the 'meal was cooked on the family's hearth and not the dhaba's. Hence, it cannot be charged for'. When I insisted, he shooed me away and shut the door again. Materially so poor he was, but he was also one of the richest men I had ever meet. Such people make one grateful for the world we live in. Who else could one take lifelong lessons from except this elder in his ruined vest and dhoti?

Strangers, friends and well-wishers have readily helped materially and morally against possible crises or harms. I have been singularly fortunate in this respect. Life has bestowed a very affectionate and supportive circle of friends and strangers—my good Samaritans. Daya bhai, the policemen at Nagpur station, Manju and Sonali, Mr So-and-So, the elderly couple of Chilpi, the elder of Marwari Basa and many more—our times continue to glow in the warmth, care and affection of such noble souls. I may not be remembering these angels each day but they continue to live somewhere in me and make life a cherished experience.

16

Tellings of the Fields

I frequently walk through the vast, vacant and rough fields of village Shahberi. They used to be agricultural fields till some years ago. In due course, they will be gentrified residential areas. Meanwhile they lie vacant and unused. Hardly a human passes their way. Occasionally, some boys come in the evenings and play an elementary form of cricket. Hidden by many trees at the other end of the fields is the village graveyard, which I sometimes pass by. A small non-descript madarsa stands adjacent to the graveyard. Between the dead and the village lie the vacant fields. Villagers have asked for a new graveyard. It is yet to be allocated. Where the dead are to be assigned eventually is in the hands of some bureaucrat living elsewhere with maps of Shahberi's longitudes and latitudes.

The fields are of sparseness, skies and solitude. They are of aimless cows, bulls, several goats, dogs and pigs. Patches of dry yellow grass grow hither and thither; an occasional mongoose runs stealthily between the shrubs that hide small shadows underneath; there is the overarching sun and the soft winds all day. The dead crow, un-persuaded by the will to be, looks askance as I walk by. The faint stench of the dirty-water drain reaches the nostrils in an inoffensive way. A pond I discovered a few months ago has a solitary man of sacred thread and chants bathing amidst frogs, algae and crowding weeds. Little hooves of goats in the soft dust intimate their bearers are roaming nearby. The muezzin's azaan from the village mosque of faded green swirls effortlessly into the sparseness, skies and solitude. A *neem* (Indian lilac) tree double bends over a garbage heap where mock-wrestle the idle and sagely bulls.

I frequently go amidst these that hold conversations of an unformed sacredness and sublimity. Of enchanting spells, they take one to other journeys and realms. Interminable, whenever I go, they are already going. They counsel; the counsel that is listened to with heed and reverence. Without being listened to thus they cannot be; nothing can be. Listening is Nature's way.

The vacant fields are not places; may be no word can be assigned to them. Perhaps they ought be called presences that carry vast absences within. Like Abujhmad. Places are man-made—bleak, bemoaning and bereaving. They do not know their malady, for without heed and reverence one cannot know. They proffer democracy, justice, equality, change, God, and compassion for the pain and suffering.

Sparseness, austerities and vacancies tell the stories that live in desolate fields of cows, bulls, dogs, goats, garbage piles, yellow grass, askance dead crow and neem tree. Their stories are of the word and wordless, the vacant and sparse. Good stories do not tell in words. A good word has a silence greater than itself. When word turns to its silence, comes the story.

Tellings of the Fields

Like the sparse fields. They are stories of silence and wordless cadence and flow. Un-silent words are strident and congested, bemoaning and bereaving.

In Bastar, when government officials came and asked for land to build a dispensary, forest depot, offices or residential quarters for staff, villagers took them to the graveyards abandoned long ago. Except the school, most government buildings were located in old graveyards; of this the officials did not know. At some places, certain incidents happened and the personnel fled. Things, however, changed as officialdoms became larger and stronger over time and villages weaker; having realized they were being sent to graveyards by the adivasis, government officials began to build offices and quarters within the village.

By design, places wreck sparseness and their fields. Places are not life-friendly. Ghotuls—one of the finest institutions of Bastar—felt violated by how places outside spoke or wrote of them as centres for indulgence of flesh and orgies while the place-less wilds held their intimacies in utmost sacredness. Bastar, and all that it was about till even the 1980s, has gradually been made into a place by the State, Maoists, Ramakrishna Ashram, Christian missionaries, academia, media, traders and teachers alike. No life is more traumatic than that regulated by those that despise, violate and denigrate it. Many plant and animal species, rivers and dialects decided to shrivel and disappear forever along with their flows and cadences, stillness and sparseness whereby people conducted their lives.

The sparse and austere comes from itself. An intrinsic cannot be conserved, replicated or communicated. Delicate, fragile and vulnerable, it can be only destroyed. It is not their svabhav to be other than themselves. Interventions are invasive and mischievous. On the way to Lanka, Lord Ram asked the sea to split and give his army the way. The sea pleaded it is not water's svabhav to split. 'That is how you made me, Lord. Else I cannot be.' Ram threatened to burn up the waters with arrows of fire. Saying that to split would be *adharm* (wrong or evil conduct), the sea readied itself for extinction. Ram sought forgiveness and implored it to raise its base for the army to cross.

I write of the sparse fields of Shahberi, of Abujhmad and ancient wilds, my childhood village, the folk, forgotten and the rest, for I go to the fields of unformed sacredness, conversations and counsels.

17

Sarup the Neanderthal

I have never seen a Neanderthal. Whatever little I know is from hearsay, odd readings and pencil sketches here and there. Seeing Sarup, however, gives the impression the Neanderthal is not truly gone.

Sarup brought my second cup of morning tea a while ago. He is always quiet and still. Whatever little he speaks, he speaks with a faintness of voice and faintness in the eyes. The lips part a little and show the teeth set apart. Hard of hearing, he speaks only so little as he hears the world. How astonishing a congruence!

I am at SIDH (Society for Integrated Development of Himalayas), Kempti. I come here a few times every year.

Of about fifty years of age, there is a slight drag to Sarup's walk though there is no deformity. There is a gentle stoop. Both drag and stoop seem as old as him; sometimes they seem older.

The softly dragging gait is as though of the Neanderthal. Stoop and drag can often be seen in the sketches of the primitive. His slow walk has a shyness as against the briskness of erect humans. The brisk and erect violate the landscape. His soft-footedness reminds one of the wilds. Abujhmadia too was soft-footed and soft-spoken, never loud, assertive or intrusive.

Sarup's jawline is like that of the Neanderthal. His uncultivated voice, a little squeaky, has a touch of excitement too, albeit faint. But there is also evident that innate vitality he and his likes have.

Much of India lived quite this way till even fifty years ago, or may be less. Although diminishing, their reminders still live in the countryside, their conversations are still held around non-issues. The pace of conversations, faintness in expressions, postures, gestures and gait suggest a timeless bearing of oneself. That is how Astu of Bastar was; the Musahar elder of Paraiyya (Bihar); elderly woman on the handcart near where I now live; or my elders in the plains of north India. As though it is the one and same living across centuries and regions. Living needed neither instruction nor learning, neither body nor soul to be known. Sarup, Astu, Musahar elder, the elderly woman atop the handcart and my elders share the same drag and timeless weariness with the world.

Sarup is the cook at SIDH. When not cooking, Sarup is generally asleep; usually on a narrow wooden bench in a corner of the terrace, where comes cool breeze from the surrounding Himalayan mountains. He rolls to his side and can fall any moment, but does not. There is a sure-footedness to his body — a quality people have lost. I remember the frequent childhood roadside play of two goats standing steadfastly on a single brick. Our bodies have millions of tiny feet. Of them are now left only two. When not sleeping, he sits on the bench looking at the mountains or at the floor where his feet stay. I do not remember seeing him looking straight ahead. There is nothing straight in his landscape. Though he speaks when the few others on the premises join in, I guess he is fatigued of humans.

In effect, there is little work for him at SIDH. SIDH also has little for itself. There is a congruence between Sarup, SIDH and the landscape of mountains. Except during the conferences and workshops when he cooks for the invitees, there is little else to do during the year. Each year, there are no more than four or five conferences and workshops; each lasting an average of two days. Whether there is only one to cook for or fifty, Sarup's bearing and pace are the same—like the moon that moves ever so imperceptibly over the mountains without one noticing. He is never without his Neanderthal drag, and stoop.

He does not know the scriptures, other texts or all that they are about. Sarup is a simple man, living incognito in the mountains. Not in wait of himself, whoever he is, he already is. There is not the exhortation to know or be himself. There is no longing he suffers from, no impulse that drives. People like him live outside of much—outside of a sense of life, of the profound and the trivial. There may not be a life better lived.

I do not know what more to write of him for we have not had many conversations; even those that we have had, have been 'trivial'—about distances to villages that are on the other mountain, the township of Kempti two kilometres away or the shortcut to it, the small river that gurgles nearby, monkeys that steal plums from the premises, snakes and his erratic cell phone (which I have never seen him using but is always plugged in for charging).

The door of my room is open. I wait for him.

Looking at him, I gather that when one is born, there are also born one's ample time and space. One needs all such time and space to live. One does not have to create or earn them. Unless they be vacant and empty, they do not remain themselves. Mediated and intervened, they become crowded and something else; as does one become with the congesting transactions for profit, power, rights, influence, moving up the ladder, etc. Sarup, Astu, Musahar elder, or the elderly woman atop the handcart stay away from such. They keep life healthy, vacant and still.

While I take leave of Sarup to return to Ghaziabad, I notice the usual look of faintness in his eyes. He does not ask when I will come next nor says a word of farewell, neither do I. Like the mountains here, he does not wish to know where I go or when shall I return again. Without looking into each others' eyes, we bid farewell in our silence and insignificance.

Stillness is without the need to move or do something. Like his hill, the Abujhmadia is of stillness. He is one with it. He is one with himself. So is Sarup with the mountains and himself. In whose companionship one can be, is virtuous.

18

Cacophonies

ONE of the abiding memories of my childhood village is that people were full of conversations that were without purpose, structure or focus. There remained a touch of the personal, warmth and informal intimacy. Their issues or size were not big. Adult or child, our world was small; too small for curiosities or to be concerned with. The world was as big as the house or the village. There is rarely a need to know a scale and size that is only as big as the human. Thence came our vocabulary and chit-chat. Stories, songs, riddles, puzzles, trails, open spaces, cattle, streams and skies were all our conversations. Yet it was as if at the back of our heads we felt securely conjoined to something big; far too big, we knew, to be found out.

Elders would indeed talk of matters like birth, death, cattle, the monsoon, economy and crop failure but their significance remained only as small as circumscribed by a conversation. They were small as an un-worried story.

I do not recollect our several aunts, uncles and adult cousins in the large joint family *discussing* matters with us or amongst themselves. Conversations was the only way everyone knew. There was not known another way of talking or living.

Legal statutes had not reached the village of the 1960s as it has today. There was the traditional and oral code. Issues were spoken of and judgement delivered in *panchayats* (traditional village councils) conversation-like, in words and sensibilities of everyday usage.

A few days back I went for the first time to the weekly market in Shahberi. It is held every Friday at the far end of the village. Over the past ten years I have frequented Shahberi's vegetable and other shops. Of three to four hours in the evening, the weekly *Shukkar Bazaar* (Friday Market) is at a considerable distance from my house. It is a good walk on a long, and largely dirt, track. Past the pond I have written of elsewhere, turning several corners upon entering the village, I asked for directions from boys flying kites and playing *gulli danda* (a game in the subcontinent, played with a small and a big wooden stick). Little girls showed their little bangles and fineries to each other. These are the monsoon months of Sawan and Bhadon. They are of bangles, swings and songs. How seasonally people feel and live! They never talk of ecology, environment or climate change. I go past a government school that I recognize; it is one that is rarely seen functioning. Many goats roam in front of the small mosque. Bhagwanna, my house help, a Hindu, lives in the mosque complex. She offered to take me to the bazaar but I preferred to walk alone. She fights with the elderly *Mulla ji* (Muslim priest) of the mosque almost every day over water supply from the bore well, the rent and other issues. 'Sometimes

Mulla ji deliberately touches, contaminates our food and runs away.' And she has another fight. But she and her husband do not change residence. Often Mulla ji scolds them for forgetting Hindu months and the customary Hindu seasonal dietary behaviours. He tells them of the various kinds of rains and how they resemble hopping sparrows, upturned or downturned elephant trunks and different kinds of croaks of frogs. He tells of other Hindu months and myths. Their relationship reminds me of my conversation with the barber elsewhere in the village. Or of my uncle and his Muslim friend from Sara near our native village.

A little towards the periphery of Shahberi, Shukkar Bazaar is spread over a large and vacant *maidan* (field). Nearby are two large banyan and *peepal* (sacred fig) trees, several other trees stand alongside. Vigorous commerce is restrained by vacancy and profitable transactions by idleness. Again, it reminds me of my childhood village, of vast and vacant spaces, banyan and other trees. And kites and cattle. What sense of the empty and plenty it gave! Nearly seventy years later, I feel the same of the maidan here. Shukkar Bazaar is of small, makeshift shacks and their people of raw ways—sitting on haunches, smoking, quarrelling and haggling over vegetables, clothes, bangles, *bindis* (coloured mark Hindu women apply on their foreheads), country pickles and trinkets. People are communicating as much with facial expressions and bodily gestures as with words. Ware in his lap, a barber sits in a makeshift chair waiting for a customer. He is as inert as the chair. A tailor waits elsewhere, for the customer wishing to fit his second-hand new shirt to size. Alert dogs, birds, cows and goats wait to shoplift off the vendors of vegetable, fruit and fish. An alert bird swoops down from a tree, pecks at a fruit and hurriedly flies back; the vendor hurls many a curse at the now airborne avian. Another halfjostles with a cow adamant on brinjal and radish. Waiting goats watch the row. Like them, two patrolling policemen pass by overlooking the scuffle. Vendors are engaged as much with the animals and birds as with vying customers. Except shaking their tails and ears against flies, the two enormous bulls stand still since I cannot say when; in their stillness bulls, barber and tailor coincide. Theirs is a resolute indifference to the goings on. Dark monsoon clouds watch from a distance. Amidst this, the mosque issues the maghreb azaan and devotees hurriedly go down on the knees. In another hour, except for the trees and emptiness, all will disappear. Each Friday much is being allowed for and upheld. In letter and spirit Shukkar Bazaar, my childhood village's maidan, and the distant villages in Bastar merge as one.

Roaming here, the short story 'Idgah' by Premchand vividly comes to my mind. I pray little Hamid and Shukkar Bazaar continue as they are.

Shortly, I turn back. Dark monsoon clouds are drawing closer. Though my bag is empty I am carrying back much. I sit on the bench near my house. A two-year-old in a long flowery frock is in querulous cacophony with her grandfather.

19

Official Woes—Of Housing, Toilets and Bullocks

UNDER instructions from above, the District Administration constructed houses of cement and brick free of cost for adivasis. Depending on the family size, houses were of one or two rooms, each room the size of an average hut. An average hut was about eight by ten feet. The government—like political parties, social organizations, intelligentsia, media, religious bodies, judiciaries and the rest—was determined to ensure social justice and ease the lives of adivasis living in mud and thatch huts. Only rarely did one come across a roof of asbestos, tin or rough country tiles on the huts. There was practically none of cement and concrete. A big campaign was undertaken by the government towards settling down the unsettled adivasis. At the same time as meetings were held at subdivisional and block headquarters, announcements were made on loudspeakers. Media campaigns, corner meetings, wall writings and other initiatives were undertaken. This was in the Kondagaon–Keshkal–Kanker areas of north-central Bastar sometime in the early 1980s. Bastar was a single district then.

Following a formal inauguration of much fanfare by the senior officialdom, and since orders from the District Administration are a serious matter for almost all of India's countryside, people began moving into the new houses. Those who did not were cajoled or pressed. But having moved in, they could not hold out beyond a week or two. With dogs, cats, poultry, goats and cattle, people began running away in the middle of night to the forests behind the hills. There they raised other villages of mud and thatch amidst trees, vines and quiet. Given the infrastructure and official reach at that time, it was not easy for the administration to chase the adivasis so deep into the forest; nor had such contingencies been foreseen or planned for. That people would rush into free cement-and-brick houses was considered a foregone conclusion. Upon running away, people were not ready to return. Gradually, the free but empty houses fell into dilapidation. They looked ghostly and haunted even to a passerby. Ironically, more than administration and the rest of the officialdom, it was the adivasis who became the butt of ire and jokes of political parties, social organizations, intelligentsia, religious bodies, media and the rest. With their oversized benign self-image, many times naive intentions are far too naive to be challenged to a rethink.

I do not know what happened to the houses or to what use they were eventually put, if at all. But there was hearsay, they were renovated and assigned as quarters to the ground-level officials of the forest department.

Official Woes—Of Housing, Toilets and Bullocks

Contrary to popular belief, governments do not give in easily on some issues; nor do others of good intent. There is the good intent but no more. Soon after the housing debacle came another scheme—that of providing public toilets. Some villages were chosen as sites for pilot projects. Each was so located that people could not have run away like they had in the case of the cement-and-brick houses. Also, the chosen villages were easily accessible and could be closely watched. Tenders were issued, contracts awarded and toilets of cement and brick raised at considerable cost. Again, the administration launched a large campaign, this time on the efficacy of toilets and welfare they bring. I remember one of the several inspiring wall writings: 'We will marry our children only in villages which have toilets.' Each of the chosen village had toilets built on the periphery. But despite educative persuasions people would not use them. Persuasion failing, and with pressing instructions from above, there came announcements through word of mouth that those who used toilets would be rewarded with a bundle of beedis (costing about twenty-five paisa a bundle then) every day. The village *kotwar* (local police official in a village) was to oversee the usage and reward details. Almost overnight people began putting the facilities to appropriate use. But soon enough, to the kotwar's dismay, even after being used, the toilets would remain dry and clean. To the administration's dismay it was discovered that people went therein with a bottle or lota of water, fastened the tin door, smoked a beedi or two from the previous day's reward and came out. Having collected their day's reward, they then stealthily sneaked into the bushes. The reward of beedi bundles was stopped forthwith. Again, I do not know what happened to the toilets or to what use they were put eventually, if at all. But the hearsay was that they began to be used as sheds for stacking hay.

For a long time it was being said by all and sundry that Abujhmad needs to be introduced to the better life of settled agriculture; that Abujhmadias need to live and eat fuller than they do by the ways of food gathering and hunting. So, to begin with, it was decided to impart elementary training to a few select villages in land use, cultivation, raising crops and usage of manure. This responsibility was assigned to the Departments of Agriculture and of Land Revenue. In the first round, the more outlying villages were chosen; they were easier to reach and monitor. By and by villages in the interiors were to be covered too. Since land was un-surveyed and aplenty in the region, only bullocks, ploughs and some rice seeds were provided as overhead assistance. Shirts and saris were also distributed for it was important to adequately clothe the people as against the loin cloth worn by men or the lugga by women. In a weeklong training camp at the subdivisional headquarters of Narayanpur, different ways of land use, tilling, sowing and harvesting as well as the use of ploughs and bullocks were explained to people. With the camp over, trainees walked back with bullocks, rice seeds, shirts, saris and a few other agricultural sundries. A few weeks later, the officials visited the target villages to follow up. They found that the bullocks and rice had been eaten away and the shirts and saris were neatly torn and festooned atop trees as respects to deities and ancestors. Many villagers had fallen ill because Abujhmadias are mostly unaccustomed to eating rice. When pressed to explain, people informed the aggrieved officials that in any case bullocks are for roasting and rice for cooking.

Schemes pertaining to animal husbandry and sericulture were given up for a more opportune time, whenever that came.

20

Four Feet of Dadangir

It must have been October. A little before noon, my back to the sun, I was sitting by the little Dadangir. The sun was now beating down less harshly on the earth. One could sit in the open for some time before needing to move under a tree. The ground was a faint yellow and pleasant.

The Dadangir was a little streamlet of no more than four feet width. Its playful blue waters ran about 1,000 yards away from my hut in Garpa.

Ambling in lazily from the northerly direction, Dadangir abruptly disappeared under the surface at the far edge of the small village, near where Burunga the Blacksmith lived with his wife and two little daughters. Several hundred metres later, it re-emerged from a vertical incline at the southern edge of the village in the form of countless driblets collecting in a small mud pool of around ten by ten feet. The pool was about six feet deep. Running its little width from the pool, the stream again disappeared under the entangled vegetation and could not be seen thereafter. About a kilometre further on in the same direction was a more or less medium-sized river. None knew where the river came from or whether it was the larger version of the Dadangir. The river was full of large weather-beaten rocks and boulders. Past them ran the waters. Many a time Suku and I would go there with knives and bamboo baskets to catch fish and wrench the crabs out of their muddy grips. We would also keep an eye out for a honeybee and sometimes we were lucky. That was the place where one late afternoon, Suku, abruptly dropping his knife, had bolted away. Frightened and not knowing what had made him run, for my eyes could not spot the honeybee in the thick vegetation, I had chased after him till he reached the honeycomb atop a tree.

Much of Abujhmad is hidden like the Dadangir, as though camouflaged. Camouflage keeps the region in a state of appearance-disappearance. The Abujhmadia senses it and does not try to understand or explain. All of the region is revealed-concealed by dense and intertwined vegetation and, at different times of the year, by mist and fog; and by the ancient dark that comes each night. Dark comes even during the day—it is difficult to explain.

The State and Maoists see it—or any place on earth—as latitudes, longitudes and data to be put to use, as do most of us. Here we become one with the State and Maoists, cartographers and data gatherers. The Abujhmadia does not put his wilds to any use.

Juru, Banda, Bulki, Suku, Sulki, Chaitu, Pilsu, Jali, Burunga—none knew where the Dadangir came from or where it went. They only knew it as Dadangir. They knew that it was of playful and crystal clear waters, and that it ran under their seven huts and reappeared briefly as a pool and again disappeared into inscrutable vegetation. That it would always be there for all amidst the seven huts. Only I would go and sit by it. I went mostly to watch the sunset. The sunset, though, could be watched from any point in Garpa. But in my experience, the sun set best at Dadangir. It went down only behind that particular western hill in the distance. Beyond the hill lay Gadhchirouli of Maharashtra, about a week's walk away. It went down behind the hill, as if on a cue, just when Pilsu and Burunga's children shrieked and played. The dust raised by their naked limbs camouflaged them. Many years later, a friend told me of the shy elderly woman in a village near Pune who spread out chillies each morning to dry outside her hut as the sun rose. When he asked her to tell him something about the sun, after much hesitation she had shyly narrated how the sun came to chit-chat with her each morning before moving in the westerly direction. It came to meet her. Such places and people ought not be converted into the lowest denominator of latitudes, longitudes, data or economic indices.

Back home, I knew where the Ganga came from, where it went or whence it flowed; its legend and stories. Or of the Brahmaputra, Narmada and Cauvery; I even knew how old they are. I knew some of the many myths and fables around them. Even though I had never even seen or tasted the waters of either. I also knew of the three kinds of Himalayas—the lower, middle and upper reaches. Or the desert of Rajasthan whose tip I have only barely and briefly seen. Or that the sun has a solar system. Now, after Dadangir and Garpa, I feel saddened by what I know.

21

Without a Story or Stride

In their coarseness, the wooden planks felt thick, fat and uncouth. I do not remember how long I had sat on that floor, but I remember that the river used to flow nearby. That was a long, long time ago. At places the planks were somewhat splintered and made noises that sounded unusual to the ear. No one had seen my head from outside for I always sat below the window. The window was well above my head. Had someone looked in from the outside he would have dismayed seeing the head cut up by the four bars. Nor had one seen it from inside, for I had never heard voices, shuffles or movements inside. I could not have seen it myself for who has ever seen his own head? But I knew I had a head; had suffered for far too long under it.

All these years I had not stepped outside the room. I could sense it was an old and large house of thick, fat and uncouth planks, of unseen bats, cobwebs and chipping walls. The room informed of its large and quiet family of several other similarly large and dark rooms, attics, alcoves, windows, verandas with broken steps, and of ventilators touching the high ceilings wherefrom dropped their withered off-white and twisted cords to the floor.

I did not want anyone to know I lived; or that I lived there. In any case, usually no one passed that way. If an occasional passerby came, he hurried past for that is how the way was. On my part, all these years I sat on the floor of wooden planks by the window and kept my head below.

The old banyan tree outside was both the elder and the neighbour. Like the rest of the house and world, I had not seen it either, for I had never peeped outside. But I could sense it the way I could the sky, solitude, river and my own life. Each place, creature or object has a sense of itself and informs accordingly. I sensed the banyan spread like an umbrella over more than half of the large house. It was so large and engulfing that sometimes I felt, the house and I lived in it. I also knew its longevity and spread by the peculiar whispers when came the winds and conversed with the leaves. Each age makes the same conversation when the winds come; for each wind comes in the same way. Often the leaves peeped through the window mischievously and told their tales in rustles. I could not understand enough but liked it in my heart.

All these years I have not seen the river, house, the banyan or the world outside. For I never strayed from beneath the window. What had I seen then? I am afraid I do not know how to answer this question. But I know that once upon a time when the house was peopled, the river had changed course; for the blood in their veins had turned pale. The river then went away from the house in the other direction. Despite that, it flowed close to the distance that lay between it and me. It now liked being by itself and unaccompanied. Sometimes I could hear the waters. Like leaves, waters say their own things too; so do the clouds, stillness and inertia. So do joy, pain, misery and solitude. They tell much. They even tell what you were in earlier times—a monkey, parrot, pond, fairy or the squirrel of five parallel lines. They had seen you too.

I could believe the stories the elders told to my childhood. That the earth and its seven sisters sit on the 4,000 horns of the cow; and that it takes 5,000 years to travel from one horn to another. That the cow rests on the Great Serpent's hood and the Serpent on the tortoise that dwells in the netherworld. That the five lines on the squirrel were made by the Lord Himself. That the earth, cow, serpent, tortoise, parrot, monkey, pond, fairy and I were all born together from our same mother. As a child, I believed, and having lived seven decades, now believe them more. That is how I wished to be and see the world and myself—as earth, cow, serpent, tortoise, parrot, monkey, squirrel, pond, fairy and I were born together from our same mother. I intuitively trusted the elders then and still do. The blood in their veins had not turned pale. There never was a questioning by me then nor is it now. Books rarely told stories, elders did.

Before electricity came, the iron lamp posts were dropped off at the wayside in buffalo carts. There lay a lamp post every two furlongs. They lay for a year or two or more. The villagers did not complain at the delay in setting them up. Gathering dust and rust, they acquired a few uses as posts to occasionally tether a buffalo or as resting places for the wayfarer. The village did not want the dark to go away soon. Electricity had too much light and possibility; such as was not needed. Too much blinds one.

Without a Story or Stride

Years after leaving the forest, one day, by the unknown ways of Fate, I reached this house of wooden planks that feel thick, fat and uncouth and make sounds unusual to the ear. That is how I came and sat below the window. No one has seen my head all these years; and these have been several years. Though even I have not seen mine, but I know I am not headless. I hide the head. I fear the seers and knowers, and the lights they have seen. Never do I raise the head enough to be noticed and plied upon. Of confident stride on an innocent earth, those of the lights are on the prowl.

I do not wish anyone to know I live here, or that I do not have a story or stride.

22

Mumblings and Miscellanies

WHAT else is self-exile? Contemporary humans are the most, and wilfully, exiled from themselves. Having allowed to be looted and marauded on the way to abundance and knowings, now we want ourselves back. Except insecurity and ridicule, what stops one from living without abundance and knowledge? Being elsewhere, other than oneself, is self-exile. Loveless selves are far too clever for their own good, or of others.

Abujhmad was particularly the 'bereft and without'; the unclothed, unsound and irreducible. For it, attire, thought, idea or language are ways to move away from living well. It speaks of abnegation of even thought and idea. In Abujhmad's irreducibility the doer disappears; so does deed. It is about the none.

Plain faith works as nothing may. By its very nature it is stupid, bereft and seeks nothing.

Only a machine can run a machine. Such are the requirements of machines. Unless one is qualified to run as one, one will not be allowed even close to a machine. An engineer is a qualified machine. Credentials attest that now they are no longer human. They can run the device diligently and enhance productivity and economy.

The irreplaceable philosophic ambivalence that comes only through 'ignorance'.

Marxism is far too energetic for the simple people of Abujhmad, or for simple people anywhere. The Marxist's utopia is as devious as the religionist's heaven.

Existence is neutral. It does not stop one from deluding oneself; nor is it affected by one's self-harm.

Absence of profession or career, relationships, broken marriage, material issues ... the list could be long. Not that they were not desired but there is needed a certain soundness and stability to sustain them and oneself. In hindsight, that unsoundness and instability were blessings in disguise. They brought Aurobindo Ashram, Paunar Ashram, Sevagram Ashram, the hard and ascetic ravines of Chambal, the barrenness of social sciences and the inscrutable ways of Abujhmad. Or those that were situated in-between the intersections. All came as good-hearted visitations but at those times, ill-prepared as I was, many times I felt torn and tormented.

———•———

Profession, career, success and singularity of purpose are not pragmatism.

———•———

Attire, thought, sensibility and soundness are the million tiny spiders of shiny black eyes that ate up the ceilings, walls, doors and floors of the rich merchant in Shahrazad's tale in *The Arabian Nights*. Attire, thought, sensibility and soundness that did the merchant proud.

———•———

So, more by default than choice, I remained a non-doer even when I should have been 'doing' and been of a little 'consequence' in my family or life. Choices are rarely made. When made, they are usually repented.

———•———

I walk another mile to look at another dirt track. In the rains, the track is inundated with water, muck and the stench of a small dead animal or two. Now dry, the grass and soft soil submerged earlier are back again. Adjacent to the track flows the big dirty-water drain. It carries its own stench. Someday I will sit on this dirt track. But I ought to practise more sitting. Sitting is hard. When I sit, the path will walk. Like it did in the landscape of slate roofs and ravines of many years ago on the banks of Kuari. Or in the conversation with the bamboo-gathering woman who said one ought do only so much as one knows; and one knows little or nothing. Time and again, when I walk myself, the path becomes a predator. The precious comes without reason or intent, will or choice. Full comes to the empty.

How the Forest Dwellers Act (2007) was applauded and upheld by those who have not seen a forest even in pictures nor have seen an ordinary landscape! Extensive naiveté is dangerous. Hundreds of seminars and marches were organized by the Constitutionalists. Empirically, the Constitutional, communal and the rest have always been alike in their understanding, value and stride. The fanatically obscurantist and religious fundamentalists in one part of the world destroy people's lives, landscapes and well-being in exactly the same way as do the equally fanatical and progressive Maoists. In both places, people either commit suicide, succumb to diktats or stealthily leave centuries-old home and hearth forever.

I wrote back saying it is sad the street dog had bitten Vikram. Canine justice? I expressed the hope both are fine and well attended to. Vikram lives in a well-endowed and premier university in New Delhi. Obviously far more endowed and privileged than the dog, Vikram now carries a stick as a deterrent I am told. In fairness, I should have also been told what the dog is carrying to similarly protect itself against Vikram. Are there some guarantees for canines too in the Constitution, court precedents, municipal laws or other such spites and prejudices of our age? If not, then what use is either? This is the paradox of these times—the privileged always complain and arm severally; and author Constitutions, laws and jurisprudence. In 2009, Bolivia granted Constitutional rights to Nature to live and continue living. Bolivia was applauded alike the world over. Nature goes about itself ignoring the catcalls, like Vikram and Bolivia. Sometimes it does not. It then bites. Here, Vikram, even though I have known him for several years, is only symbolic. Not the individual Vikram but Vikram the guardian and dispenser of rights to Nature, and who is one day bitten by a dog. Thereafter he carries a stick that does not raise even an eyebrow among the well-endowed and premier university of high political sensitivity. In the late 1920s, Gandhi ji had to write elaborately on how to relate with cattle, dogs and other beings lest Swaraj is aborted. Who did he write for? India's villages of the 1920s did not read or write, and treated their animals well. Eventually, not only was Swaraj rendered ineffectual, Gandhi ji was rendered thus too, reduced to seminars, books and readership. There has come no intimation till date what the dog has begun carrying to protect itself.

Till even some decades ago, the peasant did not take the measures of life beyond the *mutthi bhar* (handful). Till the coming of the Maoists, Ramakrishna Mission, media and the rest, Abujhmad did not take its counting beyond the five fingers.

Thoughts enter as foreign bodies and breed disease. Village elders were frightened of injections and tablets. In our vocabulary then there were not the expressions like 'I think'. How appalled would they have been at Descartes!

Just as I have not known what to write, similarly, I have not known what do with living. Both are equally difficult and alike. Running helter-skelter for the greater part of the years, I searched and searched but could not find. Till the issues themselves dropped. Then it occurred that there is nothing to find or un-find. Twelve years ago, at the ripe age of fifty-eight, I could begin to write. Many a time exhaustion and illness, failure, inconsequentiality and humiliation come by grace. Nothing that comes one's way cancels one.

Ours are now lives that have to work more and more to make themselves workable. Yet, there persists a deep sense of failure and pathos that little or nothing is working out. Without svabhav and *svadharm* (innate justness) occur irreverence and destruction of oneself and the world. There are retributions.

It needs a primordial innocence to be irreligious.

Those three shadows had come to stay. A long time went by but they refused to go. No one knew when they came, or what brought them, or whose they were. Some said they have always been there. They would appear suddenly in whichever part of the woods—by the trail or away from it, on the riverbank or inside the waters, besides a tree or swinging on its leaves. Near an anthill or within. No one knew where they lived in other times. None tried to shoo them away. They would stay and stare at the passersby. I could not spot their eyes but they stared for long stretches. If one did not move they chased many a time. Wherever they were, they became that, except the colour, which was always dark. If in a river, that stretch turned black. An anthill's red-brown mud turned as dark as its inside. The tree would look black. The trail too became dark; it was not possible to walk thereon because in the dark one loses the way. People themselves had no shadows, but they spoke well of the three.

In hindsight, a seeker is the oddest entity Existence could have. Only scarcity seeks abundance, half seeks full, less seeks more. What when there is neither half nor full or even one or none? Virtue and vice, Truth and Untruth repress one as nothing does. Whereas seeking cannot find, it helps see nothing need be sought or sent away.

———•———

I have been hearing for a long, long time that life is short. It may be thus, but I have never heard cattle, cats, swallows or others say or behave so. Even if it is short, it is not the only life one has. Many more follow, just as many have preceded. What could not happen now will happen in those to come. Were it to happen in this, it would have. More does not agree with one. It is not good to be taller than living. Let the measures not be bigger than oneself. Small things concord well with a small life: going for walks, washing clothes, chatting up street dogs, watching the sunset from the tea shack, cooking lentils, gossiping with the utensil-seller, visiting the monkey man, eating three water-balls a day, listening to someone feeling out of sorts, helping someone wanting to agree with oneself, reclining on the bed and writing something—anything that concords well with life and its smallness. So much as I circumscribe myself by the unproductive and silly, I am also that much removed from aspirations and mind.

———•———

Life ought to stay as small as itself. More is not good for well-being. Else, there would not have been forgetfulness of the self, or selfless. Both are one.

———•———

In the empty patch, some young men in their late teens and early twenties play football most evenings. Many wear blue and yellow t-shirts and shorts. One or two have stockings up to the knees. I saw a middle-aged man amidst them in trousers and a shirt. He had a stubble and looked uncommitted. Of which team he was, if at all, I could not make out. Apparently, he was not of either. His heart seemed in the play but did not seem to know what he was to do, what moves were being made and un-made, how to align himself with a move and further it, how to trap the ball or which direction to score the goal in or which not. Whichever direction the ball ran, he ran too; running, chasing and losing. Since the youngsters ran faster and had better ball control, he could not trap the ball even once. Nevertheless, running and chasing, he kept up. For him, that, that alone, seemed the play. Interestingly, no one took an adverse notice of who he was playing for or who against. After about fifteen minutes, I moved on in my walk.

Every day I keep running away from writing. It is not an overstatement that writing frightens me. Often, I look for pretexts to not write, mostly successfully. Writing is almost the last thing I turn to. It happens when options, will, intent and choice cease, and there is not much of either. When there is nothing left, I sit by. Then writing happens without writing. Sitting by is enough transaction with oneself and life. Like wild Nature, writing is inchoate and incoherent. It creates insecurity and frightens.

This ailment of seeking and knowing is very old. Knowledge has an evil eye. There are no questions and answers in playfulness. To survive despite the purposefully accumulated knowledge ought be the high ethic. Else, living is impossible.

———•———

Even if one were to seek, the sought would not come from seeking. It is likely to come through madness and stupidity. In them alone knowledge loses meaning and substance. Losing is about the only antidote to self-destruction. In the transient cannot come the intransient; formlessness cannot from form; or immanence from the immediate. Seeking is a disease of the agitated and the restless. It will come on the hot afternoon of swelter and stillness when sloth and locomotion, stillness and activity, speech and silence, meaningful and meaningless all cease and become one and none.

———•———

How scary stupidity is! There is little or nothing we have that says, 'It is wise to be stupid.'

———•———

A little bit of life we do need to live in.

———•———

We are perpetually in the search mode, seeking something that we are told we 'do not have'. Captives of the 'I am deficient' syndrome. Our language, a noisy language of a very noisy people, always speaks of growth, improvement and evolution. There is left practically no space for being without rhyme or reason, stupid or silly. Language is a carrier of ideas and their confused clamour.

Like that of the tiny 'village' of Ehnar in Abujhmad, that trail led to some 'nowhere'; one did not know where. It was so deep in the interiors; like the human heart. Sitting amidst some of the strangest country, of two–three scattered huts and miles and miles of thicket, it was not even a village. One did not know what to call it or how to know it. Or what to know of it. What does being a human mean here?

It was a cold and frosty morning. One could not see enough in that simple and intermittent plain. The trail meandered around many anthills and *dhaak* (butea) plants that oozed a milky white sap. The sap is toxic. Though anthills are made by ants or termites, they are said to be the abode of serpents. So the trail skirted round and round the anthills and dhaaks. It is not good to step on a serpent or brush past a dhaak, for both are ill omens. Beady looking, the violet buds of the dhaaks look like eyes of serpents. Very few trees, their limbs of deathly white, dotted the barren plain.

What made it a trail was not because I could see it, but because it was dusty and soft under the bare feet. When came hardness underneath, I knew I had strayed away. Then groping with the feet I returned to the trail around the abodes of ants, serpents and milky white sap. Groping was by feet for they know best. It was a strange land where eyes and ears had little or nothing to do, for there was the frost. Frost and the nebulous nullify the seen.

Utter silence has colours, of dark too. He had not tried to know where the trail came from or where it went. It was not easy to know. Who would have known in that forest of frost? Upon entering, one could see or hear no more. The fewest of sounds reached the ears. One amongst them was of the frost. How to describe it? It resembles the sound that comes from thousands of termites chewing the logs in a hut in the stillness of a night. It may also be called the sound of an ancient dark. One does not know. Though termites chew day and night, the sound comes only in the dark when all—barring the termites and their chewing—ceases. Termites chew day and night.

23

Bear Atop the Roof

It was getting to be evening when we reached the tiny village of Nelnar. That was the first time I was going there. Since walking alone was fraught with risks, Masiya had been nice enough to be my companion. It must have been something like five o'clock by the watch when we arrived. The sun was soon to go down the distant western hill. Nothing seemed to have changed in Nelnar, as though it was cast in stone.

I was walking ahead of Masiya. Child, elderly or infirm is placed in the front to set the pace for others to follow. Being the outsider, I was all three. Following the pace, the able-bodied walk behind in a file. Also, if an animal turns man-eater, a rarity, it attacks from behind. One at the rear is so swiftly and quietly whisked away that those just two or three steps ahead do not get to know. So, the one behind has to be strong and able-bodied.

Nelnar was situated in the deep interiors. Walking at an average pace, it was a day's walk from Garpa, the village of my residence. Nelnar was of three huts. They stood away from each other by about two to three furlongs. In between, and around, lay vegetation and densely entangled foliage. There was always an eeriness to the low-hanging foliage in the region. From the occasional winds came sounds I had not heard before. As sunset neared, swirling shadows began descending from the sky, bringing with them sensations and dispositions not known earlier. There came shadows within shadows. They came every evening and night. The substance of darkness emerged slowly. The darkness inside, that I had not known, began coming forth. It came night after night.

Dwellings in Abujhmad were shaky-looking structures. Generously, they can be called huts. Of low heights, they are about eight by ten feet of bamboo and thatch. There are doorframes but no doors, nor do people know of them. For want of a better word, the villages looked deserted. Often it seemed they had no occupants. Huts and humans were so camouflaged that they were barely visible. My eyes were not trained to see this way. What to the Abujhmadia was good Nature, was confounding for me. However, my eyes were gradually getting accustomed to seeing things; I was learning to keep to the trails and not deviating, never walking alone, keeping the shaman in good humour, keeping away from dust swirls, living without activity for the greater part of the day, day after day, getting used to the sudden and deep gasps during conversations (they frightened as though the listener had fallen grievously ill; the gasps were akin to the nods in conversations in the outside world), and more. Except dogs, because they barked, none seemed to want to engage with another. It had been the time of getting acquainted.

A slender and faint trail ran between the huts in Nelnar. It kept appearing and disappearing as one walked its meandering ways. Abujhmad has the endless habit of meandering, appearing and disappearing, of playing hide and seek. I say the trail was faint because it did not seem to have been much walked on and had acquired the character that less-traversed trails have. To the eyes, it was only dimly apparent but to the feet it was as if it spoke. In any case, there was much about the region that was only dimly apparent. There was not a sound in the village nor a sign of humans or their activities, or any activity for that matter. There was a stillness that would not speak of itself. Wilds are so motionless and dormant.

Many times, the wilds instilled a fear that was unintelligible. Where did it come from? What was it about? I had started to think of them as nameless fears. They had not been felt earlier. Fear, too, ceases after a point, say in the presence of a tiger or in the dead of desolate nights. After fear, arrives a numbness. But what is neither fear nor numbness may not be given to words. I could then appreciate the deep urge in humans to comprehend and make phenomena intelligible. What is intelligible is also reassuring and affirming. The need to be reassured and affirmed is human. It is understandable that anthropologists, scientists, folklorists or other experts create in the heart of untamed wilds a space for human civilization where things are intelligible, nameable and ascertainable. There is not the doubt that they indeed want the wilds to remain wilds. But that wilderness is also expected to provide for the human need for intelligibility and reassurance.

On the other hand, the deeper one went into the wilds, the less became the scope for thought, idea, discernment and intelligibility. Abujhmad appeared to be of pre-society.

Upon entering the village, to my horror, I spotted out of the corner of my eye a full-grown bear sprawled to my immediate left, no more than a foot or two away. It was at shoulder height. Such was the narrowness of the trail that I couldn't help but graze past the animal. In that moment, however, I ran as I may never have in life before or after. People said it is best to climb a tree when met with a bear; but I was not adept at tree climbing. Else, one is advised to run on a descent. The fur falling on the eyes hampers the bear's sight and speed. But there was no adequate descent in view. Along the slender trail ran the tangle of dense vegetation, at places higher than oneself. Tearing into it with the axe, hands and feet, skirting or jumping over obstacles was not possible in so short a time as a chasing bear permits. Neither were my hands and feet trained for such assignment nor my legs to run ahead of a bear to save my very life. Everywhere except the trail was impenetrable and I could have run only along it. Masiya shouted for me but I did not take heed. As the stillness was broken by the sudden commotion, village cattle assembled between the dispersed huts, stampeded and ran amidst the dust of hooves to wherever they did. Somebody running abruptly is cause for alarm. In such pandemonium appeared the villagers in ones and twos to see what was going on. Masiya and I knew some of them from earlier. I ran to them. Masiya was still ambling behind. When told of the bear, shy and gentle as the people are, they did not laugh or say much. I was provided with a leaf cup of mahua.

The moment it had appeared in the corner of my eye, there was then not a chance to have a second look. Nor does a bear allow for that; it is a very agile and quick animal. I wonder why our books call them sloth bears. My eyes could spot the large animal but not the larger hut it lay upon at shoulder height as I grazed past. Such are the eyes, ever untrained and un-adapted. Yet, ironically, we trust them as we do little else.

Soon came another leaf cup of mahua. That soothed my nerves. Chaitur promised to give tiger claws to wear around my neck against fear of animals. Needless to say, for that moment, mahua sufficed for the claw.

I was told that what the corner of my eye saw was a bearskin that Jali had spread on his thatch roof to dry out. If a bear is killed, people retain its claws and, sometimes, the skin for little children to sleep on in winters.

Such were sometimes the unforeseen hazards in the wilds.

24

'What Are You Nothing About'

My five years in Abujhmad were of 'limbo and self-neglect'. After leaving the region and coming to the adjoining villages of Bastar, a good many more years went by in the same way.

Compared to Abujhmad, it was easier to speak about the rest of Bastar. It shares, in some measure, the baggage of the world outside—human society, profit economy, industriousness, poverty, globalization, ecology, pedagogy, notions of justice, violence, conservation, health and nutrition, facts and figures—and all the familiar phraseology that goes with them.

Abujhmad seemed like a mystical metaphor for something removed and away. There seemed something indefinite about the region, as though without a narrative or phraseology. It was not of the definite, discussions or debates.

Whenever I returned to Delhi, I could not speak of Abujhmad freely with friends and acquaintances; nor could I talk about it in the seminars and conferences on adivasis, forests and ecology. Inert and inactive, in limbo and neglect, my understandings and observations about the region stayed within me, churning. I lacked that 'something' to talk. This problem would, however, disappear when I returned to Bastar. Though the Pilsus, Jalis, Tondes, Astus, Agnus and the rest were 'backward' and of 'un-vigorous' minds, they resonated deep with Abujhmad, sometimes down to the finest detail even though they had never been there. Such is the magic of contiguity of landscapes even though diminishing. With them I could frequently go into delicate detail with ease. They had only a little of the logical and rational. Nature does not allow for more. More is mischief.

Slowly, however, I began telling, mostly as little stories, some details of Abujhmad to my daughter Kunalika when she was small.

The Pilsus, Mandavis, Tondes, Astus, and Agnus sensed Abujhmad's wilds quite vividly. After all, the name (Abujhmad—'inscrutable land') itself was given by them and their likes. No other name could have been more expressive. They could understand that the wilds are not only inaccessible and formidable vegetation, hills, large anthills, caves, tigers, bears and leopards, wild rivers and streams; they are also such that the counting of only up to five makes profound sense as do facial expressions, and much nakedness. It is a region without sin, of non-doing people living comfortably without livelihood, starvation or violence. Pilsus, Mandavis, Tondes, Astus, and Agnus 'knew' instinctively that without these there can be neither Nature nor human survival.

The illiterate people of noble souls could understand how these induce a way of being of a million nuances that sustain a healthy life and healthy earth; how night and its primeval darkness are much more alive and powerful than days. It was easy to talk to them about how humans ought to neither think nor know, and that a good life ought to be animal-like. Or that home is in the outside. In their own ways, they would add to these from their own experiences, understanding and hearsay.

It was not difficult to say in their presence that Abujhmad is mostly a cadence, and that cadence can be articulated only in the nebulous and unexpressed; and that Abujhmad's nebulous may not be captured, fixed and reduced to data, latitudes and longitudes.

While we talked, the distinctions of the factual and anecdotal, objective and subjective, real and unreal collapsed. Our conversations became like stories, going into many directions and to many realms back and forth, unencumbered by purpose, understanding or knowledge. They became of fluidity. I could not have such conversations with the scholars, mystics, ascetics or holy men I had met or stayed with sometimes in other places. The Pilsus, Mandavis, Tondes, Astus, and Agnus were the ignorant and uniformed friends who had nothing to contribute to earth. Theirs were such small presences that for them nothing had to be contributed to, explained or understood. Living was not mortgaged to intent or aspiration. I knew they are a rapidly diminishing people.

Occasionally my daughter and one or two friends in Delhi would ask me why I did not write about the region.

Abujhmad provided the material but, paradoxically, it itself was not material. The first few months there and the freshness of the place gave my ignorance that which encourages material writing. In the freshness that comes from a lack of experience, my faculties were in full swing. Ignorance as such does not need ability or sense. It is enough by itself. Slowly the months and years passed and I found myself exactly where I was—not writing. Now there was neither the material nor the ability. I still had the latitudes and longitudes; and the data, facts and figures could be talked of, analysed or added to. But like an advertisement hoarding, they were shrill, gross and deficient; masculinely announcing themselves. Except for the few field notes taken in the initial few months, I could not write. It became worse when language became suspect—it could neither comprehend nor communicate the metaphorical and the nebulous. Dialect came in handy but I did not know it well enough. Also, dialect is not inclined to writing; it is less about humans and their affairs and more about landscapes and cadences.

Somehow, writing this chapter, I am reminded of a person in Sadhana village, about sixty kilometres from Pune on the way to Kolvan. He was of a differently abled mind. I had met him a few times in the summer of 2014–15. In the course of our conversations, he had once asked me, 'What are you nothing about?' I could not answer. I still do not know what he meant to ask. But the question haunts me to this day.

25

Traditional Bastar—Amongst Healers[4]

TRADITIONAL healing is something only you would know of. Had I known, I would not have come here to learn. You know healing. So I thought of spending time with you.

I do not know what to say on the traditions of Bastar. But let me begin by sharing some of my experiences about it.

By tradition, I do not mean only the healing tradition. Everything here looks like a tradition, as though the entire community is a tradition. How different it is from the world outside! Within one tradition are several traditions—a maze of sorts, just like the intertwined terrain and vegetation. Things are so conjoined. Yet so different. Even places are different.

---

[4] Translated from Hindi, this section is from an introductory talk at a Traditional Healers' Conclave at Salehbhat village, Bastar, held on 6 February 2007; initially published by *Bastar Bandhu* (25 February–7 March 2007).

Dantewada is of one kind, Kondagaon of another. Kanker is of yet another kind and Abujhmad is altogether different. That all are different is not true either. There are sweeping continuities but they are inconspicuous, as though subterranean. Subterranean continuities have no dramatic visibility. In every region here, the traditions and ways are different. The ways of living are different. Food habits are different, of worship too, so is the case with sitting and rising. Of dialects, this is more true. Gait is area specific. The feather in this youngster's hairdo tells which part of Bastar he comes from. There are shapes within shapes and smells within smells. Everything is so different, yet alike. There is something that joins the vast Bastar together.

So, what is the tradition of Bastar? What did it look like, and still does? Can one even see it? Is it visible? What are its features and attributes, arrangements and apparatus? When I first came here some years ago I could see Bastar's tradition. What you eat, what you wear, your customs, rituals and manners of doing things. The architecture of your houses and households. Also, governance in villages, the role of village elders, eminent men and women, the shaman and what he does. I could see the socio-economic structures and the impact of outside economies and polity, and so on. Gradually, however, I felt here there is more to it, more that is not dramatically visible. That behind this visible Bastar are the relatively untouched arrangements and assemblages of its wilds and their emptiness. There seems a severance from the contemporary outside world. Something that lies outside the bifurcations of the individual, family and community, outside of animal, earth and sky; as though outside of the bifurcations all are one and the same. Bastar helps one sense that.

The architecture of this house we are sitting in, your attire, eating habits, social structure, non-profit economy, gender relations, notions of proximity and distance, all has come from the wilds; they are not simply man-made. You have not intervened in them and neither they in you. One way or the other, the life of non-intervention continues. Interventions are coming from the outside here and, as one sees around, Bastar is rupturing too. Yet it is still lingering on in many shapes and forms and at one level or the other. Gradually, it became clear to me that 'tradition' here is not man-made, not something intervening and impinging on Nature, something that moulds or modulates, but an extension of your wilds. Abujhmad's lesser vocabulary and speech, quiet dialect, limited counting, ways of worship, gait and body postures, the very few quarrels and their resolutions, procedure of decision-making in the village, absence of the notion of freedom, justice and equality, ways of condoling a death, architecture of the hut and village, disease and healing, textures of relationships with gods and goddesses, ancestors and spirits, all come from the wilds. In the outside world, 'tradition' is understood as something made or modulated by man. Here, tradition is letting the wilds stream into your lives.

My stay in Abujhmad had been a few months old then. I used to be confused about the place. One day I asked the elderly Banda why along with several dogs, cats, poultry and goats does a family stay crammed in a tiny hut of about eight by ten feet? Each night about thirty beings sleep crammed together. Over and above, space has to be left in the middle for fire too. Why does the Abujhmadia not make bigger huts and homes? Bamboo, wood and thatch are available freely. There is no government presence nor are there laws to curb people. There is no restriction on felling trees nor on occupying large patches of land. Banda heard me out and said, 'Home is in the outside. It is endlessly large; how can we make it any larger?'

After those few months of my being in Abujhmad, I could not see that they lived in what for me was the outside but home for them. Their cooking, eating, drinking, sitting together, conversations, weddings, procreation, birth and death all happened at 'home in the outside'. Banda had further added, 'The hut is only a shelter for the night. We do not lay much store by the hut. In the immense dark of night, tigers, leopards, bears, spirits, gods, and goddesses roam in our "house". So we then move into the hut till sunrise. In turn, they move into their "huts" at sunrise. Making way for each other, we all live in the same house.'

It set me thinking about myself. Although I was there as part of a research project to study the Abujhmadia, now it became more important to study myself, the times and society I came from, its sensitivities, worldviews, values and ways of looking at itself and others. I believed 'home' was inside; that is where I had lived my life till then. Much store was laid by it. But Banda says it is in the endless outside where all are housed. In the morning, 'I will leave the hut and return home.' For the first time, I stood bared. I had not been able to see what was obvious and visible each hour every day. I had heard from the loin-clothed Abujhmadia what I had never imagined or heard elsewhere. It perplexed. More than a place, Abujhmad became a presence. All of Bastar, particularly Abujhmad, is a suggestiveness. It is of a vast nebulousness. It was the beginning of an enduring relationship.

I will not be able to speak on the healing traditions of Bastar. Only you can. Mine is no more than a sharing of my experiences of here. So, tradition here seems to mean concurrence and coherence with wild Nature, the landscape. That is the source, ends and means. Not just trees and plants, all stand included in such concurrence and coherence. That which is seen and that which remains unseen. Gods and goddesses, tigers and trails, spirits and ghosts. There are waters, winds and earth, too—the counting may never end. The ability to concur and cohere with such endless and countless, in every given moment, is Bastar. In their alikeness, it is not easy for the eye to discern where the contours of a human body end and that of a wild bush begin. A man is sitting under a tree, entangled vegetation surrounding both. Man looks like the surroundings, the surroundings like man. The architecture of your huts, villages, trails, healing, artcraft, consumption and conservation, distances and proximities between villages, non-profit economy and the rest are quite like the man under the tree—of concurrence and coherence. All come from the uninterrupted and un-modulated. Such tradition, it seems, cannot be man-made.

In Abujhmad, a hut has a doorframe but no door. They do not know what a door is. There is no means of opening or closing the hut's entryway. Open always, there is nothing that bars or bans entry into the hut. So, the tiger passing by at night about three times a week can come in, so can the bear, snake, scorpion, ghost and evil, winds and directions too. None is shunned. 'I will think of a way of protecting myself but I will not refuse.' 'This is allowed, that not'—such a view of things does not exist. None is denied. Animals, birds, plants, trees, the directions, gods and goddesses, ancestors … all have the place and possibility of coming in through the open doorframe. That which is of here and that which is not of here—all have the same place and possibility. For centuries, outsiders have come and settled down in the rest of Bastar. The potter, blacksmith, woodworker, monk, weaver, wanderer, artisan, trader and many more came. Bastar gave them the same place and possibility as belongs to it. They settled and came to belong here. So, in the small portion of earth of my village and hut too everyone ought to have the same. There will not be the door that opens for some and shuts for the rest. I have to stay here, so do others. Those that I like and those that I may not. That which is manifest and that which is not. Past, present and future, sun, earth and sky, life and death too have to live here. None is refused. Of same kinship, inclusivity and fullness, were one to live well, such a principle in Nature is inescapable. Such a worldview is often not seen elsewhere. This vast imagination of life and land, and uninterrupted kinship with it, I saw only in Abujhmad.

That is also how the healing tradition appears to be here. You have learnt healing in Bastar and not from outside. Incantation, exorcism, blowing wind in the ear, healing herbs and plants, conversing with stones, the sky and space, conversing with spirits, bone healing, curing paralysis caused by shadows of birds and snakes dwelling in the Pandki tree, healing the conflict in 'turned minds'—all this you learnt in the soil and mind of Bastar. This is not to say that doctors from outside have no place. They are here; adivasis are seeking treatment from them too. They access treatments in hospitals too. But what is the difference between the one growing out of native soil and the one that has travelled from another source? How do they respectively look upon illness? What are the assumptions in understanding illness, patient, healing, life and death? Who is the healer? Is healing possible by sidestepping the virtue involved in healing?

Sometime back I was speaking with a healer in the village Bheja. He is the younger brother of Jungloo, the healer. You know Jungloo well. He said healing systems from outside cure sometimes; sometimes they do not. Patients die too. Even after treatments in good hospitals by good doctors, they may die. That is how it is in traditional healing. A patient may die in the care and treatment of a traditional healer. The patient may be cured by both or he may die with either. Per se, there are no good or bad healing systems. But there is a difference. Suppose someone's kin has to be admitted to a hospital. In the first place, we do not have the money needed for treatment. Even in government hospitals some money is needed for travel, medicines, meals and various kinds of running around. Many minor things must be done. Sundry personal expenses—like on tea, beedis and betel leaf—are incurred by the family members and caretakers. In case of the patient's death, doctors say, 'Take him away. Vacate the bed or floor. Other patients have to be admitted.' If there occurs a delay in this, they scream at the family member and even use abusive language. But some delays do occur. Death of a kin is the time to grieve. All over the world, when a kin passes away, it is the time to grieve. That is what people everywhere do. But the doctor says carry away your dead and vacate the place. Instead of crying, one has to begin making arrangements for money. Bills have to be paid. The deceased has to be taken to the village. Hiring vehicles is expensive and ambulances are missing or unavailable. The hospital staff is screaming, 'Take him away. How long will he keep lying here? How can the hospital run thus? Take him out.' Both the relative and deceased have to suffer much hurt and humiliation. In our healing system, the healer stays with the departed. He accompanies the dead till the cremation grounds. The dead is not parted with till he returns to the elements he had come from. The healer must accompany till then. This is the Dharm of healing. This is also the Dharm of the healer. Both begin in Dharm.

In those few words the healer said much. Healing continues till cremation. The departed is not to be expelled or shooed away. The five elements make up both the living and the dead. Neither is a waste to be gotten rid of. The healer accompanies the deceased till the departed becomes one with the elements.

26

Trail and the Writer's Chore

Stories from *Chandamama* had drawn my attention quite early in life. *Chandamama* was my first introduction to happy reading. Gradually I felt that imagination happens not just to the mind but also to the known or unknown—many places and things, and in many ways. *Chandamama* helped one effortlessly and purposelessly cross back and forth the many magnificent worlds without making one feel out of place. Expanding and contracting, they were worlds without a centre and of fluid boundaries. There came the feeling, and conviction, that outside the explicit reality is a far more intimate and palpable one living expansively every moment, moment after endless moment. It is outside of the contemporary. By and by, the contemporary seemed municipal, far too deep in reverence of itself.

A couple of decades later in Abujhmad, as in many other regions, I found that dances were performed around a centre.

They were performed in a circle. The centre was usually marked by a piece of rock, a wooden peg or other such denotations. The centre could be placed anywhere on a small patch of land on a given day. It could be moved to elsewhere, too; and the dance would continue around that new centre. Irregular and wobbly in circularity, the centre remained unfixed and unfirm. Both centre and periphery could move back and forth. They were accompanied by a one-line song of varying pitches and intonations accompanied by similar beats of drums. The song was of two-and-a-half words *Rela Re Rela*. The words were repeated ad infinitum, till the dancers felt like or till the moon of inaccurate orbit came overhead. In the region's small vocabulary, *Rela Re Rela* were more than words. They were sounds without meaning or substance. Just themselves, they were like the rest of Abujhmad—without meaning or substance but with fullness of the void. In the circularity of dances and songs lay their vitality. They returned to where they had begun from, to begin yet again in the same endless intonations and variations. Similar were the Abujhmadia's stories. They were of four or five lines. Without seeming head or tail, they ended with a seeming abruptness. There was not the conventional closure to them, nor the willingness to proceed further along a potential sequence. Like everything else, the story was not entitled to finish itself. Stories were ways of living that the teller and listener treasured. Of inexactitude and inaccuracy, that is how the Abujhmadia's speech too was, comprehensible yet with a hint of abruptness.

In the primitive wilds, nothing may greet a life more than its own and else. That which is and that which is not, both were equally existent and revered. Such was the paradox and inexactitude to the Abujhmadia's perception and understanding. Such also brought back for me *Chandamama's* stories of fluid boundaries where much could be. That is why the Abujhmadia's body contours merged with the bush. The unfirm and uncertain looking hut merged similarly with the surrounding landscape. The tentative-looking architecture of huts has remained thus the Abujhmadia did not know for how long. That is also how he did not place himself at the centre of the wilds and claim them as his own even though he shared an indivisibility with them.

That is the writer's sole task—to speak of own and else. It is also the writer's task to move towards his or her own and else sans which writing may not be. One that neither 'is' nor otherwise. For that is how wild landscapes and their people are. That is also how they go about their rudimentary and simplest of lives. The elders in my childhood village would believe the starkly opposite in the same moment—that which was widely accepted as true and that which was not. They would believe in the same breath that the Big Canal in the village had different origins in different regions, often far flung from each other. None had cared to explore or see. All opinions were believed in the same breath; that is how our young minds were fed. Or the *bahroopiyas* (impersonators) who came now and then and pretended to be who they were not, Lord Ram, landlord or police officer amongst others. Village took them at face value and accordingly conducted itself in that moment, though knowing they were only impersonating. Villagers of Dedhuki in Saurashtra (Gujarat) performed stories from the Mahabharat on Dussehra even though Dussehra is related to Ramayan and not the Mahabharat. Although it surprised me, but not for a moment did the villagers wince or question. Neither did the elderly and destitute Musahar adivasi of Paraiyya (near Gaya, Bihar) question although he had been waiting for a roof of his own since his grandfather's times of 1948. Despite eligibility under government schemes and several visits and petitions to concerned block-level offices, his grandfather could not get the government to give him a roof available under the scheme, nor could his father, nor he himself. It was a wait of over seventy years for a roof. His son, he says without lament or protest, is unlikely to get it either. In everyday mundane conversations in Rajasthan, when one does not know something, for example, the name of a tree, the reply is, *'Mainne thah koni'* ('I cannot fathom it').

In daily conversations in the adivasi or folk communities there is implicitly, however indirect, a reference to the formless in a given form; as though each is without a centre or periphery. There remained a dissuasion against precise and efficient articulation, one that makes 'sense' in the circumstance. There was a lurking avoidance. Conversations were sprinkled with metaphors that left behind trails of suggestive meanings but rarely a fixed one. That allowed for an irregularity. Negotiating in faint words or no words, revealing and concealing, is a prospect that languages in the world outside may find difficult to make much sense of. Of different hues and flavours, I think such avoidance and austerity, at one time or another, have been shared by many communities across the world.

Unless living and writing enmesh, there may not occur either. The writer ought to write to the edge of irreducibility; so ought his or her life live itself out.

Like each life on earth, each trail in a landscape is of irregular territory. Each territory has its trails that lead elsewhere. Each remains uninhabited, without a map, latitude or longitude. How can it journey to the wrong place when begun with itself? Even though the way may seem wayward, it is the way home.

27

Writing as Municipal—Word, Landscape and People

A word is as much, if not more, made up of inarticulation as it is of articulation of that which is lurking in an un-intervened landscape and its people. Though the writer longs to but feels incapable of articulating fully. It remains unsaid even after the writing is over; and the writer looks on helplessly. Hence, as though to catch up, one writes more. Each successive piece is an attempt and each a failure. For the writer each writing is a self-admonition of sorts.

Word has a cartography and structure—fixed and authoritarian—like all structures. Only dance, poetry or humour assuage it to some extent. Unless corresponding to dance, poetry or humour, writing leads both writer and reader into the factual and false.

Writing as Municipal—Word, Landscape and People

Writer and writing are quintessentially civilizational; structured to the extent that both are unnatural too. How then ought the writer communicate the wordless Nature and its people? How to speak of the obscure and intangible that over the years has gone round and round inside? Or is it even required to write of it?

Having had an association with the adivasi and folk communities, I have wished to also speak of things that may not make much sense; things that have an intangible, wishy-washyness to them. In the outside world, theirs have neither much significance nor weight. But they, nevertheless, have lurked in regions and their people's lives over generations. How to write of still locomotion, silent sounds, small vocabularies, bovineness, self-denial and disinterest, absence of aspirations, living by the measures of handfuls, and the rest that nurture and sustain them and the landscape?

The written word is of a mould. It has an intention. It is as unnatural and civilizational as thought, sensitivity and history. To write of the wordless, mouldless, intentionless and unintelligible is a predestined failure. It is a deep irony that the writer tries to word the wordless. Writing ought to be about irreducibility to the point of wordlessness and nought. Unless the writer's own life too thus reduces, writing may not be. Nothing may manifest it better than landscapes of nought and wilderness. They are wordless. The writer ought to write to the edge as though it is the nought and not writing happening. So ought life live itself out. It is not that life is one thing and writing another. Ironically for the writer, word is the only means he or she has. Ironically, again, word is also amongst the least expressive unless its object corresponds to intention and mould, viz. of meaning, substance and civilization.

The adivasi or folk do not write of landscapes or wild Nature or anything else. Nor did they devise a destined-to-fail vocabulary for this neither may it be devisable. They only live in Nature, not with Nature but *like* Nature. To break out of word and articulation—of intention and the intelligible—is breaking into health; in other words, to break out into the uncivilizational. So far as I could gather, for the adivasi and folk articulation or intelligibility of phenomenon is too material and municipal to live with.

Wild gives its dwellers repose.

28

Tin, Tarpaulin and Bamboo Poles

I sat under the bridge. It was barely inches above my head. Over the bridge went the river with its waters. Two fireflies flitted without weight or force around what must have been a large boulder. Their circular motions indicated that the boulder was circular too. Flitting, they provided light and disclosure, so much as was sufficient. The bridge was of thin and interwoven bamboo strips, some in decay at the edges but still sturdy and flexible to bear the running waters. Waters went across to wherever waters go. They go somewhere as do winds, directions, times and minds. Why be curious? I was there only to sit beneath. Only when one sits beneath does one sit. Sitting, I remembered curiosity used to be a bad word in my childhood village. They used to chide us, 'Why are you being curious?' We were children, playful and light-hearted, but were chided if we were curious. Curiosity was akin to being trivial. For all and sundry, living came from our still and bovine landscape. We began to learn sitting beneath and the ethics of such sitting. So I was not keen to know where the waters went or why over the bridge.

When my family moved from the village to the town, I became more of the school and of much else. I learnt to sit atop the bridge. Whereas earlier I drew with my fingers the trees, ponds, canals and barad in the kheda in the dust or made cows, buffaloes and carts of freshly fallen barad leaves, now I drew continents, oceans and the solar system that I have not seen to this day. Over time I forgot the fingers, trees, ponds, canals and barad. There came countless curiosities that went beyond the reaches of our homes and landscapes. Eventually, it turned into a journey to homelessness. To cut the long story short, by a quirk of Fate (for what else could it have been?), I happened to reach Bastar and its Abujhmad. Slowly, the eyes began opening to what had hit, and what had been hit.

So, well past sunset, I sat under the bridge where the fireflies provided light and disclosure so much as was sufficient; and over which went the waters to wherever waters go.

People have always seemed curious. They are of ardent verve and locomotion, as if they will die tomorrow; maybe tonight. Scarcity of time, space, health, resources, love and much else plagues them. They seem homeless. Homely people are of stillness. People of trees, ponds, canals, barad and kheda did not have locomotion nor issues, concerns and drives that power them. They did not allow themselves to matter much. It was a life in health, love, conviviality and much else. Fireflies went round and round without locomotion. They hid and came forth, hid again and again came forth. Thus, it went. Thus, they lived.

There was the cinema hall of tin, tarpaulin and bamboo poles in the mofussil town of Janjgir in Chhattisgarh.

Tin, Tarpaulin and Bamboo Poles

After Puducherry, Paunar, Sevagram and Chambal I happened to live there for some time. In the cinema hall one had to put one's feet up on the squeaky tin chairs for beneath chased several cats the several rats on the earthen floor. Ancient and noisy projectors sent the round beam onto the cloth screen fastened between bamboo poles, and all came alive. Mosquitoes, other insects and dust particles made the most of the beam of light. They managed to be seen on the cloth screen along with the charming actors and actresses. The screen fluttered many times in the wind, and the faces that momentarily turned different caused guffaws. When came a song the audience sang along. With that entered the tea-sellers with improvised canisters containing burning twigs to keep the tea hot in the aluminium kettle, samosas (delicacies made of savoury pastries stuffed with boiled potatoes and spices) and 'time pass' (peanuts). Songs in the film were considered brief intervals of sorts. From the outside came the loud chatter of other peddlers selling country delicacies such as roasted grams and spicy puffed rice mixed with a touch of mustard oil or strips of dried raw mango and jaggery. A cow mooed outside as she went by. It was the circus of life enmeshed with un-sanitized ordinariness of everyday living. When the electricity failed, came grievous lamentations. After a brief wait, I headed home on the bicycle of many colourful embellishments rented from Chhattisgarh Cycle Store. Of greater patience, many others waited even though everyone knew that it could take the electricity an hour to a week to be restored. In their native wisdom, none grumbled, protested or asked for a ticket refund. Films were called '*khela*' (play). Like life, it was play, ever changing and unworthy of longevity or abiding trust. It was taken lightly like the circus of life. People watched films the same way as they lived their lives.

The mofussil stayed only as large as itself.

They were ordinary films like the ordinary people's town of Janjgir. Full of dialogues, songs, chatter and other sounds, those films were the khela of keeping the hidden hidden. They were about the less and finite in an ominously expanding world bent on knowing and articulating more and more. The new world needed more—more feeling, more thinking, more sensitivity and more space, time and doing. Being less is rest and repose.

I wished to hear that story of rest and repose again. So, I sat beneath the bridge which hung barely inches above my head and over which went the waters to wherever waters go.

The khela of tin and tarpaulin, rats, cats and feet on the chairs, boulders, the bridge above, narrow roads and donkey carts, Abujhmad, my village, the barber and his tales, Saurashtra's Dedhuki, the woman sitting atop the handcart, Astu of Bastar, the elder of Parraiya and maulana of the tea shack are the stories of rest and repose. They are one and the same story. They help against the baggage of meaning, substance and growth that crowds my story. So crowded that it took all of Bastar—a region larger than Belgium—and some years of stay to remind me of something as elementary as my own simple story. Something so integral had remained absent for so many years. Instead of crowding, they provide only as much light and disclosure as are needed. Hiding and coming forth, they hide again and again come forth. Thus, it goes. The bridge lies overhead and over it lie the waters that go to wherever waters go.

29

Atop the Graveyard Wall

As the crow flies, the graveyard is about half a kilometre from where I live now. Were one to walk the trail, the distance is about a kilometre. Eventually, however, one is not expected to walk there by oneself. It would astonish and unsettle a lot.

It is evening. Shadows are descending stealthily.

I sit on the graveyard's four-feet-high boundary wall. It is dilapidated and dusty, of falling bricks and chipping cement. The place does not look inhabited. It looks more abandoned than inhabited, though inhabited it indeed is. How deceptive habitations can be! Like their dwellers, the dreary earthen mounds lie hidden under shrubs and tall grass. Amidst, hide snakes, scorpions and the mongoose of hurried gait. I sometimes come across the mongoose on my walks. On the mounds stand several neem trees, some deviously twisted owing to age and intent. Silent shades of their foliage are of a sweetness that many may not know. Atop the neems perch a few crows, unspeaking but agile. It is still and quiet, an uneducated quiet. Nothing speaks nor is there the rustle of whispers. There is a mood, palpable but indecipherable. But there is not the ruing and melancholy, neither the mourning or remembrance nor the sanctity associated with the dead and their graves. Going by the ambiance, the dead are as ordinary as those alive; no more no less.

A thin-looking man of deep-set eyes, long green shirt and a dusty white beard—possibly the *goar-kin* (gravedigger)—reclines on a string cot. He looks towards me atop the wall but does not enquire of my business. It is not unusual, in any case, to be sitting atop a wall. His equipment, a pickaxe, shovel and spud, rest against the trunk of a tree—a little concealed by the bushes and grass. Much in a landscape is a little concealed and a little revealed. Atop the mound of a grave recline three goats in the manner of the goar-kin on the string cot. They are lazily stretching their legs. Another stands on the hind legs, plucking leaves off a shrub higher than her stretch. Two dogs roll about playfully on the ground; the smaller has the bigger's ear lightly held in its jaws. An old, accursed-looking rusted wheat thresher lies in a corner next to a stump; either in eternal rest or for safekeeping by the villagers against thievery. Large and sprawling shrubs of acacia spread around for several hundred metres. At the entrance of the graveyard a stone plaque announces '*Qabristan*' (graveyard) and '*Aram Gah*' (abode of repose) in Urdu and Hindi scripts. A handwritten placard makes known 'Others Not Allowed'. Hence, I had come to the back of the graveyard and sit atop the wall. Much sitting, reclining, inactivity and stillness live here.

The wall is lesser by many bricks. There are many a gap here and there that the nearby village dogs, goats and other smaller animals walk through without noticing the handwritten placard. Someone may have taken away the missing bricks to add to his own house of scarcity and shortfalls. Maybe that is how, sometimes, houses and much else are built. The dead do not notice, not even when they are alive.

I shake my knee.

A madarsa hides away amidst the tall shrubs and neems at the far edge. What better place for learning? Here alone can learning happen. It happens, if at all, in quiet and concealment; unnoticed.

I return to the nights in Abujhmad of some forty years ago. One way or another—I cannot say which—there was nothing in those nights of primordial dark; nothing that was in, nothing that was out. There was not even the sky above or ground below. One could not see even one's own hands and legs. The utter dark strangely concealed and revealed simultaneously. Nor was there any telling of the day from night. The day had the sun but the sun was dark. It was the un-composed and un-attributable dark. The region was of a 'without' and vacancy; one that does not distinguish day from night, one from two, virtue from vice. To say that the dark 'was' would be far too misleading, stemming from folly of language and understanding. It was far too immense and overwhelming to be described as what was and what not. That was neither stillness nor cadence, neither sound nor soundlessness. The wilds' utter unknowability is inscrutable. That is how here it may be under these raised mounds for those who are no more nor were.

A hush comes to the ear. I cannot hear or comprehend. It is neither hush nor whisper. It is the only thing that both violates and speaks the stillness. What is it? I cannot say.

I have walked past this graveyard several times over the years.

Abujhmad is no more, it never was. It is not to be searched for. Only that I did not know. By the time I left, it had become for me more a metaphor than region. It is in each. It happens on its own, like sight, touch and breath. Only I did not know. One who does not know, gropes. One who does, also gropes. Abujhmad has reached this graveyard too. That is how I now sit atop this wall. Like the mounds, crows, goar-kin, goats, dogs, mongoose of hurried gait, and thresher I do not enquire of the business of life or death; nor did Abujhmad of me or itself. Now I sit atop in quiet.

Along with the graveyards of Bastar and elsewhere, that is how this graveyard reaches me. Places reach. This is how, some decades ago, (late) Binay Singh, my acquaintance, too had reached me. He and I had sat the night in the Christian cemetery. He had to be sent to his native village in Bihar for his last rites. Sitting atop the wall here, I remember the companionship that lasted a night between a living and a dead.

A village in Bastar

A hut in Abujhmad

Inside the hut

A ghotul and hut in the process of construction

A bird loft

The cottages in the village

Sunset near the river in Abujhmad

Khasgrass (scientific name: vetiveria zizanioides)

The local musical instruments, which are slowly disappearing from practice

Gond Muria boy

Gond Muria girl

The villagers performing the jungle dance

A scene from the village meeting

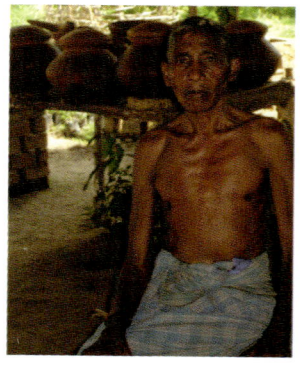

A local from north Bastar

A man breaks into an impromptu dance performance

A child shaving the twig with a sharp tool

An artist focusing on creating the local artwork

A young man practicing bow-and-arrow skills

Madia Baba

A man lighting the fire for a prayer/ritual

The sacrificial fire for the ritual

Preparing for the sacrificial fire

The deities

A man drinking the locally-brewed drink, mohua

Scene from the weekly market in Bastar village

A man making the pills out of natural elements

River Disappearing into the Rock Cave

A view of a hut, central Bastar

30
All Said and Done

Quite incapable of a career or earning a livelihood, I have lived with much time at hand. Despite what is disparagingly called 'unemployment' or 'under-employment', my body and soul have stayed reasonably together. There were family, social and economic pressures, at times severe, but somehow earning a livelihood could not find an important place in the scheme of things. It was not out of some heroic idealism. Suffice it to say I have found myself unequal to doing many things in the life lived over the past seven decades. I am, un-embarrassingly, made that way and have not been in much conflict with it. Even when badly needed, it was well-nigh impossible to go contrary to my make up. After returning for good from Bastar in 2013, writing and doing small jobs here and there is about all that I have done. In Bastar, even this was not done. Till about four or five years ago, there was occasional project work on adivasi issues, some editing or translation work now and then, delivering a short talk in a university, institute or elsewhere or assisting in organizing a conference or two on themes far removed from my interests. Whereas earlier there was much travel, gradually it became occasional. From these sometimes came some money, sometimes not.

Over the years, there has been the almost unfailing afternoon nap and sleep by ten at night.

But all that is now no more. No more are there the invitations to talks. I liked delivering them, especially when they involved students and other youngsters. Invitations stopped because maybe the talks did not communicate much. Now there are minor household chores. They take away some of my time, but I do not mind. For the rest of the day, I am left with myself. In the evenings, I take to walking through Shahberi's large plains or its dusty winding lanes; or have a cup of tea at a shack facing large green agricultural fields. The fields have scarecrows and a handful of thatch huts with goats at the other end. Or I meet the cobbler, barber, utensil-seller, tailor or the maulana. As mentioned elsewhere, the maulana is ever disinterested in running his small tea shack and his bearing shuns the customers. It is his disinterest and aloofness from customers that I find the most endearing. Else, I go past the temple where sits for alms the old monkey man with his two mischievous simians. Stopping by for a small conversation, I give the primates some money to buy two bananas. Sometime ago, the monkey man had only one monkey with him. I enquired of the other.

'He has gone to our native village.'
'Gone to native village?'
'Yes.'
'What takes him there?'

'He has work.'
'He has work?'
'Yes.'
'When does he return?'
'When the work is over ... maybe in a few days.'

I was not sure whether he was talking of the monkey, some relative or a son. Or whether it is the way of talking about animals with whom one has lived for long. I did not have the heart to enquire what business had taken the monkey to his native village about seventy kilometres away or how it travelled or with whom.

People used to suggest I ought to be realistic in life. They would often ask 'How will you live?' I did not know then, and I do not know now. In the meantime, a good fifty years or more have gone by. There have been the highs and lows a human is subjected to. I do not have a dislike for realistic living. But I have always felt that I am realistic enough. When it comes to important matters I, usually, do not quarrel with the gut. It was a fairly early feeling that living a lesser life is living a more realistic one.

How language changes its tempers! Till even fifty years ago, there was not the word 'livelihood' in our vocabulary. In north India, it was called *guzaara* (etymologically meaning a sense of passage). The usual question used to be, '*Guzaara kaise chal raha hai*' (How is the passage going)?

Ambitions or aspirations are always larger than one, else they cannot be. They do not exist in reality but are creations of the larger social mind. Ever since they have come, their promise to help exceed oneself has been enticing, even compelling. Being unambitious or unaspiring is not a heavy demand on oneself or another; projected realism is. Giving much, if not all, of oneself to something that is not one's own—own size, own little worth—or is of an external value is severely unrealistic. After all, the purpose of livelihood, if one were to determine it, should be no more than a healthy togetherness of body and soul. Such togetherness remains even when there is no livelihood. Living must be reduced to its basic ordinariness—something we have been fighting against with extraordinariness.

When one is born are also born one's time and space. One does not come so empty-handed as is usually said. For a simple and healthy life, one needs all the time and space created for one. Unless kept empty, they do not remain themselves, but are mediated and intervened. One crowds them and oneself with much that is extraneous—some of which, if not most, is rubbish. That is what the times want to take ownership of—time and space intrinsically given to one—and deliver the congesting traffics of growth and transaction. We need all our intrinsic time and space to do little or nothing.

Writing would not have been possible for me were it not for the less work and much time. The 'less' would not have been possible. Less is what happens in abundant time. It needs more time. Writing may not be the best thing I do but it is the least thing I do; although it is my heartfelt wish to do still less of such little.

Living on the edge, staying away, is not an abnegation of realism but the very substance of it. Each moment life lives at the edge. It knows better.

31

Vultures in the Sky

EXCEPT within the village of three–four huts, it was forbidden to move around alone in Abujhmad. On a whim, that day, I had decided to go for a walk in the outside. There was not the wish to go far nor did I have the daring. I decided to stay within shouting distance. A walk, in any case, was an oddity. People did not go for walks in Abujhmad.

It was a cold wintry morning. There were no unpleasant insects flying in the sky. The sun was pale and the mist heavy. Dawn brings its own conditions, when the things are just beginning to reappear from darkness and are still unreal. In the distance stood blurred the dark hills of immemorial times. The sacred saja tree that stood ten steps away was a hazy blur that would clarify itself within the hour. Little Dadangir was no longer watered by a sparkling blue. It was now a meandering length of thick and rising mist ambling through the pristine vegetation covered with the tiniest of droplets, adding to the blur that rose from my feet to the sky. It was mist from horizon to horizon. The slender trail ambled languorously towards some nowhere, its eventual destination obscure. Everything was obscure. Wild obscures all phenomena. Dewdrops carpeted the grass like a million pearls, each reflecting a million dim suns. I stood amidst a dazzle disguised by the carpet of mist. Some disguise—self-disguise no less—is needed for living, some inexplicit for well-being.

Such are Abujhmad's mornings. Velvety to the senses. This certain obscurity in the landscape is the very skin that conceals much. Mornings cannot be otherwise here. Mist and blur are their skin. One cannot take off the skin.

Apart from an occasional red jungle fowl there were only vultures that floated languorously round and round in the sky. Vultures have an 'ominousness' to them. Theirs is the menacing task of tearing apart dead creatures. They also serve to inform that a tiger, or an ill omen, is on the move. Increasingly smaller and smaller circles of flight tell of a somewhat precise location. Sometimes they squeal repeatedly and communicate the location more emphatically.

In the small bag slung from my shoulder was a small tobacco pouch that Juru had made for me from a spherical root of a tree. It was only a little bigger than a poultry egg. Beautifully carved with a hot knife, the pouch could be held in the palm. But I wanted my palms and hands free as one of their favourite pastimes is to hang loosely. The Abujhmadia tucks his pouch in the single fold of his loin cloth on either side of the waist. Similarly, the woman does so in the fold of her lugga. Since I did not wear a loin cloth, the pouch was in the sling bag.

Walking lazily, I noticed two large and dark eyes peering from the bush. There are hardly any bushes in Abujhmad. What I am calling a 'bush' was a thickly intertwined and large clump of plants, creepers, stems, leaves, cobwebs; and perhaps with a dead creature or two inside. In the intertwining, it holds itself together. Sometimes it forms around a small abandoned anthill or a fallen tree trunk. Using them as a base, the bush grows around them. The eyes were turned in my direction. I looked at them in the dark of the bush. The cheer in me vanished for they looked unusual. I do not know how I felt in that moment or how long the moment was. Benumbed and stupefied, and even if the thought to turn back and run had struck, I couldn't have. Also, the dew-laden trail was slippery. In any case, running is not advisable. One has to stay still and wait for the circumstance to change.

Hardly had I stopped walking when there ran out from the bush a small and hazy figure towards a large moss-covered boulder about a hundred yards to the right. There form no dark shadows when the sun is pale and the atmosphere is heavy. Yet, the figure's shadow was dense and pitch black. It ran hard and hit the boulder with equal hardness. In that instant, it disappeared into its own shadow. It was no more and seemed to be hiding within the shadow. Perplexed, I did not know what to make of it. Two men came rushing into where the shadow was and poured *gorga* (toddy) from their small gourds into my mouth. The vultures circled above in the sky. They were narrowing their circles but not climbing down to the location.

The two men began walking me towards the huts. They were Dunga and Pilsu. I had not told anyone that I was going for a walk. I do not think they had followed me. Had they been following, they would have come from the direction of the village where I had come from. Instead, they had come from the opposite direction.

Never did I ask about the incident of that day, how they had suddenly appeared or what the shadows were. Nor did they tell. Some things are best left to themselves. Never again, however, did I go for a walk.

32

Inner Journeys, External Mappings

A friend of many years has on a few occasions suggested that my writings would be more grounded if some details of an autobiographical kind were mentioned, such as details from my childhood and adulthood; people I met and how they influenced me; why and how I reached Bastar, Abujhmad and other places; and the choices that got made—the inner journeys amidst external events.

Though in some measure writing becomes necessarily autobiographical, it remains ever unnerving. Many such vanities and conceits come to the fore that one would never wish to see in oneself.

It is not uncommon to sometimes think how else could one have lived and made different choices. Many times, I have thought why I had left college prematurely, or gone to Bastar and Abujhmad. Before going there, or to other places, most places were those that I had neither heard of nor could locate on a map. Needless to say, I could not have thought of the people I met and their abiding influences on me. Much in life happens on its own. Puducherry, Paunar, Sevagram, the Chambal region, or eventually Bastar and Abujhmad happened on their own. There is no explanation more honest that I could give myself.

Temperamentally, I am not given to actively engaging with or initiating things. Mostly, I have let situations happen and lead me. Waiting for situations to occur comes naturally to me. I am a waiter. I have always felt in the gut that that which is effortless alone is abiding. Reinforcement of such a temperament came in due course from long experiences with the adivasi and the folk. There has been an inborn weariness as such; to each, blessings come in disguise. I do not remember having short- or long-term goals. Goals or plans become difficult when one cannot engage actively.

Abujhmad and Bastar alone are not the issue. Living cannot be contained in one place, experience or thought. As much as Abujhmad stands out in my mind, so does the intended one-month walk that began out of despair from Puducherry to Kanyakumari, one that got aborted overnight; or the sheer placidity and uneventfulness at Vinoba's Ashram where much of the time nothing seemed to happen; or to that *one* moment (how moments, so fiercely footloose and independent, cannot be anticipated) I first saw Subba Rao ji in the foreground of a setting sun in the still ravines of Chambal Valley, digging with a spade into an earthen mound on the outskirts of the village Modhana Jawahar. I had never thought someone who had so completely turned the hearts and minds of some of the fiercest baghis could be so ordinary and commonplace. Or, when I saw the baghis themselves whose uprightness and nobility was straight from the fables; or when the farmer friend's wife in

Inner Journeys, External Mappings

Baghchini village, despite knowing her husband of thirty years would return before sunset, had replied '*Ko jani,* (who knows when he comes!)'; or the moment when elderly Bulki said, 'No sin can come to Abujhmad;' or when I heard Astu's axiom that the earth is only so big as it appears in one glance; or when Banda said that anyone who loves Nature is an adivasi, that there is no ethnicity to being one.

I do not know why but these moments have deeply held my attention and they could not have been planned. As though with a momentum of their own they meet one suddenly in an instant somewhere. Amongst these I had longed to be since childhood and for which the bridges had been burnt.

Yet, in themselves these external events—places, people or experiences—may never explain the inner journeys of the obscure, dark and nebulous, of countless paces and directions, of muteness and shrillness simultaneously. These may never be known to me.

Paradoxically, the attempt to make oneself destroys one, and one becomes one's own victim. It is like self-cannibalizing. To make oneself is a rational and heroic choice. But to not make such demands, in contemporary times, a self-decapacitation of a fairly high order. It asks for a certain dismantling, disordering and infirmity within. These, too, are blessings. I found that this is how people in our villages lived. Their folk and mythological tales to such ends were heart-warming and profound. Insofar as they spur such dismantling, disorder and infirmity, tales are often hard taskmasters. Also, they help spur and see the dismantle, disorder and infirmity from another vantage point to another end if there be an end. Blessings come in disguise.

Mostly, life keeps to its own subterranean course and trajectories even when it seems to be going nowhere.

After leaving college around February 1975 and whiling away time for over a year, one day with a ticket and fifty rupees that my school friend Arun Saxena gave me, I reached Madras (now Chennai) by GT Express and thereafter Aurobindo Ashram in Puducherry. I had come to the Ashram because there was no other viable place I knew of to go to. The Ashram inmates were kind. After nearly a year's stay, I reached Vinoba's Paunar Ashram. Living in his presence was one of the finest graces I received. He told me to graze the Ashram cows for six months because, as he said later, I needed to cultivate patience. What better way than being with cows!

It was at Paunar I first heard of Gandhi ji's Sevagram Ashram. It was ten kilometres away by the dirt track. Since my early years, I have held the great soul in the fondest regard. I still remember walking those ten kilometres and the feeling of a purifying pilgrimage that had come over me upon seeing his little mud hut or the little round seat and backrest (made of a bare plank) he used for the evening prayers. Almost everyone at Sevagram had either been an associate of Gandhi ji or was a Gandhian of deep earnestness. Being in the presence of such people, awed me; just as it was in Vinoba's presence. Many Gandhians from different parts of India and elsewhere came visiting the Ashram for conferences, workshops or other purposes.

With Gandhi ji's weighing machine keeping watch from the corner, Sugandha tai (over forty years later I may not now remember the name correctly) kept track of the Ashram kitchen stocks as meticulously as Gandhi ji himself. Whereas meals were free, a glass of milk cost a rupee. One day Mata ji (Nirmala Behan Gandhi, Gandhi ji's daughter-in-law and wife of his son Ramdas Gandhi) enquired why I did not drink milk. I told her how I could not afford it. She asked me to visit her hut after dinner. There I got a glass of milk every day and occasionally a papaya or mango that grew in her small backyard. Thus began an association that was extremely rich and educative. I received first-hand information, opinions, thoughts, feelings and anecdotes about the Mahatma that could not be easily obtained from elsewhere. For example, that Gandhi ji visited Mata ji, Ramdas and the children practically every evening (his own hut being about 200 yards away). I saw the corner in her hut where he took off his wooden sandals; the wall he leaned his lathi against; how he played with the little boys and girls and humoured them; his impersonations and pantomimes with them every evening,[5] where he sat and dictated or himself wrote countless letters to the powerful, mighty and ordinary. I found these details as profound as his Satyagraha for without them his almost all-inclusive political movement may not have been. In due course Mata ji wrote a letter to my mother assuring her that I had not strayed in life. Mother treasured the letter as she would only a few other things but continued to worry to the bones about me.

A year later, with travel fare from a Gandhian institute, I went to Subba Rao ji's Ashram at Jora—Alapur in the

---

5   I have often wondered if I, shy and withdrawn as I was, would have had such a warm and rewarding relationship with Mata ji if I had the one rupee to fetch myself a glass of milk; or if I would have been privileged to hear all the little anecdotes about the Mahatma. Or would Manju behan and Sonali behan (at Paunar Ashram) have opened the Ashram gates at 10 p.m. for me—a moneyless stranger—when the Ashram inmates were already well into their 'midnight' sleep and eventually let me stay there for a year. Or would I have spent my first night by a tumultuous sea and been hosted by an unknown village when I started walking towards Kanyakumari because I did not have the train fare. The list is long.

Chambal ravines where the experiment of baghi surrender was succeeding. The baghis, like Subba Rao ji, were men of high moral stature. Had they not lived by such virtues, the surrender of such fierce and daring people with a legacy of 800 years would not have succeeded. Their ferocity notwithstanding, I had not seen such people in flesh and blood earlier. A year and a half later, and an unfortunate misunderstanding with Subba Rao ji, I left the ravines. Paradoxically, it made me understand him better and my respect for him multiplied manifold. It is not easy to understand a saintly soul without much patience and passage of time.

I returned to Delhi for a few months. Not knowing what to do, I took up miscellaneous jobs like delivering industrial oxygen cylinders to small factories and workshops in a truck or delivering duty-free goods to embassies from an authorized agency. Less than a year later, in 1979, I was in Bilaspur district (then in Madhya Pradesh). It was there I first saw adivasis and heard of Bastar. Bastar was about 350 kilometres away. Soon enough, I was there on an invite. Till then, I had not heard of the inscrutable land called Abujhmad. Five years later, in 1985, when I came out of it, I had lost whatever little marbles I had gone with. To come out of there with marbles intact would have been tantamount to returning empty-handed and not worth the salt of the Inscrutable Land.

The fisherpersons' village between Puducherry and Cuddalore that sheltered and fed me that tumultuous midnight by the sea, or the two ashrams of Paunar and Sevagram, the ravines and baghis of Chambal, or Bastar and Abujhmad or the numerous other villages, people and situations, or the countless conversations, rhythms of everyday living and the numerous disinterested faces with a sense of the transient and ephemeral—all came into my life practically on their own.

All through the years I did not feel like coming back to Delhi for good nor was it possible. It neither was nor is still advisable to live with the back door open. When faced with a crisis (of which some were grievous), back doors can be enticing. I was not, nor am now, a strong person neither do I see much virtue there. Those energies are more conducive to other things.

Till a couple of years ago, some college, university, school or institute would invite me to give a talk on adivasis, ecology, biodiversity, learning in Nature or some such issue. I do not understand these in the formal or academic sense. So I talk experientially and conversationally. Conversations do not objectivize or subjectivize. Sometimes they are objective, sometimes subjective, sometimes both, sometimes neither. Like stories, they happen in freedom and may not be planned or structured. Many times, they become goalless. They can be on a specific theme but happen outside it. Playing, they can digress to a seemingly far away issue and then return. Like an anecdote, there is to them an uncertainty and tentativeness. They can include what would otherwise be left out. For example, 'biodiversity' seeps into all areas of a village's life. For the adivasi and the folk, biodiversity is incomplete without dances, songs, stories, gods, goddesses, sayings, examples, jokes and witticisms associated with trees, bushes, vines, animals, humans or the rest of the landscape. That is how a people relate to surroundings and environs and compose biodiversity. Without inclusivity and humility, biodiversity will not be. Its subtleties shape architecture and relationships. Ceilings and doors are kept low so that one enters one's house with a bowed head. There are other beings living inside—ancestors, the ten directions, gods, goddesses, memory, winds, earth, space and nothingness. So, it is not one's house so much; one is only sharing it for a brief while and far down the lineage. However, now the invites from the educational institutions do not come. Seemingly, after the talks, the audience has not had much to carry home.

Some might say I romanticize the village and the folk. I can only say that the village, wherever it survives with a landscape, is not a mythical construct. Along with what it is, it is also a human longing for the rhythms and flows, paces, conversations, vocabulary and cadence that till recently constituted our lives and affairs. Such is an India we no longer talk about. Rarely does a book or seminar mention it.

Having already travelled over three-fourths of life's journey, I am beginning to remember the blessings of my parental generation, *sukhi raho* (live in peace and contentment).

33

Thieving the Beggar

IF memory serves me well, it was at Shahdol that a hobbling old man in rags and with dirty matted hair boarded the train. A Sikh couple with three small children sat on the berth opposite mine. I remember them because I could not smoke in their presence. Each time there came an urge, I went to the door. The year was probably 1986.

The old man was a beggar. He came from life's hard ways. Life treats some very coarsely and one may never know why. I was travelling from Bilaspur to Katni and thence to Jabalpur. All three were part of Madhya Pradesh then. That was before the formation of Chhattisgarh in 2000. Bilaspur to Katni is one of the most picturesque stretches of rail travel through some of the thickest jungles. There come several wild rivers, waterfalls and endless thickets of dense vegetation beyond which rise many hills of ancient times. Denuded and weather-beaten, the hills have turned dark.

Hobbling from berth to berth, the old man went around imploring one and all for alms. Deftly clapping two small pieces of asbestos in his fingers with chipped nails, he was hoarsely singing a hymn to their beat. Some gave money, some ignored, some shooed him away. When he reached our berths at our end of the coach, the Sikh gentleman offered some coins. I, too, put a fifty paisa on his wrinkled and outstretched palm. He then sat down on the floor where our feet rested. We shuffled our feet to give space which he in any case would have taken possession of, such being the ways in our trains of lesser prestige and privilege. Also, generally, passengers in such trains do not take seriously the issues of reserved or unreserved journeys. Space to sit is more important. The unreserved intrude and occupy berths and places wherever and however they can. Sometimes it involves a plain request (usually met out of a sense of consideration, albeit unwilling) and at other times there is some pushing and jostling. In some cases, there is a mild fisticuff wherein the passenger with a reservation may be physically dislodged from their seat. That the rightful owner holds a reserved ticket and claim to occupancy, and the intruder not even a journey ticket, is not always a legitimate argument. 'Everyone has to travel to one's village; it is as important for the unreserved or ticketless as it is for the reserved and ticketed.' That the coach is only for passengers holding reserved tickets is not always a moral basis for settling disputes. In their bureaucratic pragmatism, the railway's ticket checkers usually keep away from these trains. People's will prevails.

Frequently, goats, dogs, calves, fish and poultry travel with their owners to small and big markets in our villages and townships. Human or livestock, neither has a ticket. The smaller railway stations dotting the countryside often have a flavour of the village common space where people gather for chitchat and village gossip. Life adapts in different ways.

So, having collected alms, the elderly beggar came and sat between the family and me. By the looks of him, he was unmindful of either. While he sat, he kept scratching his beard or drinking water from a chipped ceramic bowl. Occasionally he looked around, but at no one in particular. Soon enough, he decided to lie down. His head went under my berth and feet under where the family sat. The torso that lay in between looked headless and legless. The family and I let him be.

Needing a smoke, I took out the cigarette packet from my shirt pocket. As I rose, out came a fifty-paisa coin. It fell, clinked and rested near where the old man's knees were on the floor. As I bent down and picked it up he brought out his feet and head from under the berths, sat up and took out a tattered pouch from the waistband of his dirty rag of a half-dhoti. Counting the coins therein, he repeated the exercise a couple of times. Then tucking the pouch back into his waist, he looked at me and said, 'Return the fifty-paisa coin. It came from my pouch. You have stolen my money. There are witnesses.' It was an unexpected turn of both the event and the coin. I could let him have the lucre but his accusation, manner and tone were clearly an affront and ill-treatment. After all, I had let him sit, lie and feel comfortable in a space to which he was not entitled. Now he was accusing me of stealing. Since he was an old man of life's harsh ways, I told him the coin was mine and had fallen from my shirt pocket. Disregarding that, he again asked for the coin and began calling me names. His voice was turning rough and harsh, and gesticulations threatening. There was a commotion and people from the nearby berths turned their heads and looked amused. The Sikh family stood by me and told the elderly man that the coin had indeed fallen out of my shirt pocket. He, however, would not relent. Whatever the error in his counting from the pouch, he was convinced that I had thieved him. The more time went by, the more dauntless and accusing he became. Affronted when I did not relent, he lay down in the earlier fashion. This time, however, he clutched my ankle which was next to him on the floor. His mind made up, in no way would I be allowed to escape. Now he threatened, too, that when the next station came I would be handed over to the police. My ankle would remain in his grip till then. With a body part thus clasped, I couldn't have a smoke. Since I did not want to create a spectacle more than what already was, I let the ankle and the grip be. Even though old and infirm, the clasp was resolute. By that time, I too had decided to call the police at the next station.

After about forty-five minutes, the countryside began opening up. From the thickets we were now out in open plains dotted by houses here and there. Upon seeing the limestone processing plant, I knew we would soon be at Katni. Known for lime production, Katni is a small town with a fine railway station. Torso in view, the old man was still under the berths. Apparently, he did not know that we would soon be reaching a station.

Spotting a policeman, I called out through the barred window. Before long he was next to us in the coach. Baton in hand, his khaki exuded the dominance servilely accepted in our lesser trains. By that time, the old man had come out from under the berths. I recounted the incident to the policeman and how I was being accused of stealing and how the old man was not releasing my ankle. The beggar gave his version of how the coin fell from his pouch and how I had pocketed it, and how he has been holding the ankle for law to take custody of. Despite the Sikh gentleman's arguing on my behalf, he was still adamant and saying I should be tonsured and paraded on the platform. He had now begun laying curses on me and the Sikh gentleman. At that point, some of the fellow passengers vouched for what I had recounted. Soon enough, the policeman picked him up by his arm and led him out to the platform. Only then was my captive ankle released more by the force of authority than a change of heart. The amused onlookers had sided with me, the Sikh family more actively.

I am certain the elderly beggar continued to believe I had thieved him and must have laid many an additional curse on me. But such were the circumstances both he and I found ourselves in inadvertently. One may never know why. Most of the times in life, people are blameless. Inexplicably, situations just conjure up.

But at no point did a fellow passenger accuse him of being ticketless (which he indeed was) and intruding into a reserved coach, that he had no business to unlawfully trespass there. The grievance was against his harassment, howsoever inadvertent and misplaced, of another fellow passenger. The grievance did not pertain to laws and rules of travel not even to the fact that he had encroached on a reserved space. Such are the ways in our trains of lesser prestige and privilege.

Something was owed by everyone to the old man in rags and dirty matted hair without ticket, food or money. Coming to know our people and police so much as I have over the years, I felt assured that given his age and condition he must have been let off almost immediately. Praise be to the policeman and the passengers of our lesser trains.

34

The Illiterate World

How does one see the world? Is it important to see it? Or even possible?

Childhood was the time when, in a manner of speaking, the village and its little world were opening up to me. Looking back, it was a significant time for me. Later, we siblings and our parents went back there during school and college holidays, or sometimes in between too.

The village was like any other in the region, maybe even the country. There were what are *now* called the caste Hindus, Dalits and Muslims (these words were only little known back then). I only faintly recall one Brahmin family in a population of about 2,000 families. We had many Muslim neighbours; we never called them Muslims; as mentioned earlier, our word for them was 'Seik'. They were weavers, blacksmiths, carpenters, agriculture workers and others. 'Muslim' was a very rarely used word. Depending on their age, we addressed them as uncles, aunts and grandparents or by first names if they were our age. We greeted the Dalits similarly.

Though only sixty kilometres from Delhi, historically the national capital, our village had not heard of the Buddha, Shankaracharya, Ashok, Aurangzeb, Jinnah or the rest. But Tulsi, Kabir, Akbar and Gandhi had reached somewhat. They were talked about in conversations, though very rarely. Delhi was not important to us; also sixty kilometres was a long distance then. People were mostly concerned with and talked about the village and region. We knew little of Delhi or the rest of India. Villages had a way of insulating themselves and guarding their nativity and well-being.

Some time back, a friend sent a review of a book[6] on what happened to the Hindus in Pakistan—how the 23 per cent in 1947 have shrunk to less than 3 per cent now. I have not read the book, but have access to some passages. This chapter is based on that review and the passages. Such alone ought not entitle one to talk about a book. The review and passages do, however, provide substantial clues to how and what the book is about. Also, it triggers thoughts in one that may, at times, be outside the book's purview. Going by the review, the said book is a scholarly work. Much of the socio-political scholarship since the partition of the Indian subcontinent does not acknowledge in a substantive way the ordinariness of people that the event affected the—ordinariness of their daily living; how their apparently divergent details of religions, castes, ethnicities, dialects and conversations were so intimately interwoven into a reasonable and functional coexistence without many hitches.

---

6   Farahnaz Ispahani, *Purifying the Land of the Pure: Pakistan's Religious Minorities*, HarperCollins India, 2015.

Much of the said book is about social and religious categories and not about people. Categories that separate people while people in their everyday interactions are about interweaving and coherences. In one way or another, it nurtures and reinforces the secularism of social sciences, yet another arm of the State.

They were Muslims, we were Hindus. Though there were two schools in the village, my preceding generation was largely illiterate. None of them had read our respective Gita and Quran, nor any socio-political treatises. We felt no less, or more, Hindu or Muslim on that account. Though we were not so driven by our respective faiths, we still were good practitioners of everyday living. There was much more culture than religion in the region. Religion did not have primacy over native culture. Not knowing much beyond the village was our defence. The fact that we were Hindustanis (Bharat lived in the scriptures, in the minds and writings of the educated classes and in the Indian Constitution) formed a substantial part of our consciousness. But primarily we were of our village. As I have mentioned elsewhere, I had not heard of Pakistan till I was a good twelve years old; even then I did not adequately know it implied living separately.

Our learnings came from the conversations of our grandparents, uncles, aunts, parents, neighbours and others, as also from our landscape of limits and finitude, slowness, mutualities and coherences. Our beliefs and practices about ourselves were not sanitized, nor were they so about others. There was retained a certain nebulousness, an undefined, as though deliberate. That left open many possibilities, including witticism, and the under-use of beliefs as well as what is now termed 'identities'. Beliefs remained light, just like life, to be lived and not died or killed for. Conversations were not engineered, nor issues and concerns manufactured, nor our vocabulary doctored. Even when I became aware of Pakistan I did not know that the word 'Muslim' means being so different. People did not read newspapers or books and were not aware of the issues they raised. Of course, there was the radio; it provided much homely entertainment and only a little news. For around the past twenty years, again I have not read newspapers and, for the same reasons of engineered conversations, manufactured issues and concerns and doctored vocabulary, I do not have a television; nor do I read books except those of children's stories.

Like most books, the above-mentioned book's tenor, concerns, language and emphasis are those that we had never known or lived with, even though the book is about us and the likes of us. Nearly 90–95 per cent of the subcontinent's ordinary people will not understand it just as they do not the holy scriptures, the Constitution, judiciary, parliamentary democracy, electoral processes, institutions, national budgets, secularism or other such frameworks of State–society systems. They are a non-stop seminar about India and Pakistan. They speak a different vocabulary and sensibility ever larger than our lives' ordinariness.

It may be argued that I am talking of a past, a nostalgia; but past and nostalgia are categories of the modern sensibility. How easily we get usurped by the artificial. I prefer to be anchored in the continuities of the past rather than in the contemporary framework of homeless realism.

I have talked of my childhood village and its region, of our shared land, ethos and landscape. That is the best I could be said to know.

35

Un-Noticing and Unheeding

AFTER we left the village, I remember how enchanting our returns with parents during school vacations were. Once I joined college, I began visiting by myself. After that the visits decreased and practically stopped for a long number of years. Gradually, the village disappeared from my mind.

It was in Bastar that the village began returning by and by. Those memories began coming back almost pictorially. Whereas Bastar perplexed it also helped rediscover my village. It added to the village and brought a mist that I could not much see as a child. The village took on new significations. There began coming a subtler and greater intimacy with it now. I was revisiting it in my heart and mind.

One was a reasonably well-to-do agricultural community and the other a forest adivasi people. Their physical settings were different but were marked by an identical ordinariness of life and similarity of rhythms. In any case, there are no marked differences in the ordinariness or rhythms of people anywhere unless otherwise presented. Both had a similar pace of daily living, similar forlornness to the ambiance, similar afternoons stunned into stillness, similar world-weariness and sense of passage, limits and finitudes of human knowings and reaches and a similar drowsiness to architecture and village layout. That similar effortlessness could be smelled in the winds. There was that sense of austerity and sparseness that spreads across all of India's countryside and binds it together. A ghost lived in practically every household, a god or goddess too, a fairy or two came during the nights to the pond, or a fiend lurked nearby after sunset. Bastar and my childhood village lived the similar. Amidst such, there was some un-concluded to both. Separated by about 2,000 kilometres and of much apart eras they inhabited, the two shared some boundaries going through each other seamlessly. As time went by, it was easier to see more of one in the other. That the adivasi and folk are different was turning out to be yet another myth. My learnings from earlier had not revealed or taught this about regions and people. They could not penetrate the veils behind which Bastar and my village had been in conversation over the centuries; each receiving the other in concordance and conviviality.

About three months ago I was walking by the temple. It is close to where I now live in the suburbs of Ghaziabad. Devotees were entering and exiting with that purposefulness, hurry and chaotic efficiency one sees every day in our jostling surroundings. The earlier mentioned monkey man sat outside the temple for alms with the stillness and abandon of a sage, neither in a hurry, nor with purpose or intent. Coming from another faith, he could not go inside nor did he allow himself it seemed. Once the devotees came out of the temple the faiths mingled. In the name of Lord Hanuman, the monkey God, they gave alms for the monkeys and him while children played with fellow primates. Children and monkeys are always playing, though none is a player. Playing happens without players. There is something of the inscrutable at work. Differences between them do not exist nor matter unless otherwise perceived. There is much intermingling behind the veil.

Here at the temple, I come to see both, the playful and the sage-like. Like the village and Bastar, only the playful and the sage-like are together. They are of the one and the same. Here, if there be any who impel they are the monkeys, monkey man and the children; none asking the gods or life for anything, none giving anything either. The rest are disturbed and disturbing, of a helpless death-wish and prayer. I thank the temple gods for bringing the monkeys, monkey man and children lest the temple depletes. Play alone is the temple's sacredness.

He reminds me of stories. On first seeing him about ten years ago, I had felt he has reached here like a story—wandering and mingling like my village and Bastar. He is of a tale. He is a tale. He drifts, as though all over, and weaves into that which village and Bastar converse about in concordance and conviviality. There are no eras or differences severing him from himself or the earth. Of around seventy years, with a flowing and untidy beard, a rag around the head, a tattered kurta and a faded tehmand, and eyes that cannot see enough, he is without despair or cheer. He senses the world but does not allow it to penetrate him—'I am complete without it. It cannot complete me.' It is a repose that comes through distancing and withdrawal or it comes through grace. Looking at his recline and face it appears he does not have a livelihood. The two monkeys are fellow pilgrims, not livelihood.

Un-Noticing and Unheeding

Like stories he gallivants. Like the nomadic Pardhi community ('bamboo people' in Bastar), who encamp at the edge of the village where the village and world meet, he wanders at the periphery of life and the conscious-unconscious. He is Astu the ascetic, the homeless Musahar elder of Parraiya, Sarup the Neanderthal or the village of Dedhuki in Gujarat. They twist, turn and swerve all, and themselves too.

I call him a story because a story is the entirety of one going to the entirety of the other. He does that. Else they would not mingle. While seeing him, a story is being weaved within the seer too, sentence for sentence, word for word. It is weaving together the inside-outside of both. There is a togetherness to him that makes the one half heard, the other half unheard, but the same. That completes this elder monkey man's tale. That is where he and the seer meet; that is where everyone meets, all meetings happen there.

Wandering from mouth to mouth, without purpose or pursuit, the stories of *The Arabian Nights* reached Hindustan and joined the conversation of my village, Bastar and the monkey man. And like him they struck an instant chord—the man and tale resonated. He, *Alibaba* and *Vetal Pachisi* turned into one. Premchand, Intizar Hussain and Gabriel García Márquez become one; they are one in the elderly monkey man.

Like stories he does not allow for questions. No questions are asked of the teller.

36

Many Walked That Day

THAT was a long, long walk. One that walked on and on. It had begun when the day began. When the day began, I do not know. When I began, the day had already begun. Because many walked that day, I too did. There could not have been another reason. Many a time one does what others do, like with food, clothes and habit. I asked some. None knew when the day had begun. Everyone walked the way of the slender trail that went wherever it did. Many walked thence where the way did. I did not know where it did. Neither did I ask nor was I told. It was not the day of askings or tellings, of findings or knowings. I could not see the trail nor feel under the bare feet. But trail it was, for it took many a turn and twist, many a descent and climb, many an abrupt clime; as does a trail.

There were other trails. How came this one, I do not know. Most remains unknown.

It was roofed with a dark—a moonless dark that paradoxically illumined that day under the sun. Sun and day they were but they were dark. Day comes from sun but dark from itself. But it was the day of which wayfarers knew not whence it came ... or went. Day it was, but of luminescent dark. As were the nights in Abujhmad's little village, Ehnar, of three bamboo huts and a thousand fireflies. Luminescence swam across the earth in that elemental dark. Nothing was of the eye except the forest aglow. Ehnar's nights were darker than the dire but not dismal.

This day of dark roof too was dire. But not dismal.

There came a heap at a distance from the way. I looked at the distance that walked up to it. The silhouette sat upon the distance. What else was there to sit on? Of what was the silhouette? Beyond the distance, commenced the farther. The farther was not in distance. It was exempt. It was right under my feet, those that I could not feel. Farther was of itself. How else to say it? Distance was dark but not the farther that lay right under the feet. Exempt, it was neither illumined nor dark. How to talk of it? It was without entity or attribute. This time I looked closely at the distance upon which sat the silhouette. Whence comes distance, also come silhouettes. It went up to the heap. The heap sat atop itself. Seamless heap sat atop itself. What could it be? I had never seen such in that long walk that walked on and on; one that began before the day had begun. I needed rest. I wished to rest atop the heap that sat atop itself. But could the feet bring me back? When the feet had dropped away, I could not know. The trail remained underneath. I walked on it as did the rest. Many a time one does what others do like with food, clothes and habit.

I looked up at the roof of the dark. It was of a thousand fireflies. Then down at the trail. Then at myself. Nought I knew. None was capable of being known. The knowable has to have entity and attribute. It was like little Ehnar and its Abujhmad. They were there but their knowability was amiss. Both were without entity and attribute. In Ehnar the thought that seeks to know, or any thought, had no relevance or task. Thoughts are tasked, most times like menials. So dark, irreducible and thoughtless it was that no knowable lived there—only the Abujhmadia did. The conjured alone can be thought of and known. God, democracy and freedom are the conjured, weapons to secure the known and enclosed. Ehnar lived un-conjured and unencumbered. It lived in the farther and exempt. God, democracy, revolution, freedom did not exist nor the social, legal, economic and spiritual or their thought. Primeval landscape was without substance. Unknowable. Nothing there begot a thought. To conjure are needed other conjurings like human society and civilization—village, town, city, country, community, substance and system. Of three tiny huts, Ehnar knew none. I remember that first journey from Garpa, the village of my residence. It was a dawn to dusk walk on the unused trail in eternal sleep and still. That is how trails are. That was the first time when midway—in midmost of that primal landscape—the trail seemed to say it may or may never reach Ehnar. Pursuit, walking and their reaching seemed inconsequential.

Like its dark and luminescence, human and hill, tiger and tree were indistinguishable, so are substance and civilization. To seek substance is to found civilization. Ehnar lived in the outside.

That writing or phenomena, like much else, has to be knowable and intelligible is an error that even devoted writers ought not commit. Writing is not supposed to speak or reach or even start. Or devote. When of an end or cause, when of entity and attribute, of head and tail, then it has the responsibility to be intelligible and civilizational; devoted and committed. Then it ought reach. No longer itself, it has then to necessarily become them. Such writing is hinged to understandings and explanations, conjurings and substance. Intelligibility is a premised societal condition, circumscribed and settled once and for all. For such writing to be, there has to be an agenda— the agenda for human living. It has to be human-centric and agenda-driven. Else such writing cannot be. Agenda conjures the rationale for living, well-constructed and waylaying. Else, writing is like the little tale of four lines in Abujhmad, without head or tail, end or means. It is the unhinged, adrift and aimless vagabond; of elemental disorder, unintelligibility and vagrancy. It comes from itself. It is of itself. Itself it is nought.

Here, it is not my inclination or task to understand or explain writing or its phenomenon, for I do not understand. If you understand, you have been waylaid. In writing, I ought to go where the vagabond goes and stop where it stops.

Ehnar and its Abujhmad lived as bearers of insubstantial life; and related to it no more than that. For the institutionalized human like me to be a mere and mindless bearer of the insubstantial is the most difficult to be, for what then becomes of meanings, values, ideals and aspirations? Of the immense project of love, compassion, justice and equality, violence and virtue? Even though none of these exist except in the conjured and societal. Human life is raised upon the conjured and societal. Take them away and the human condition collapses. To Ehnar, meanings, values, ideals, justice and compassion are an encumbrance and rejection of life and soul. They congest. The world outside is the bearer of much revered refuse. It parasitically lives off those that do not exist; nor ever did. How can the human be of health and life then?

Unknown to it, Ehnar is what the world of sum and substance would deeply be ill at ease with. That which is without sum and substance is considered a disorder and desecration. So now have intruded the hand-in-glove Maoists, the Ramakrishna Ashram, State, trader and intelligentsia, revolution, God, democracy, knowledge and compassion—each with unprecedented virtue and violence. They embed the conjurings in the adivasi who does not conjure.

Let me hasten back to that way which none knows where it began. Many walked that day. I too did. Many a time one does what others do like with food, clothes and habit. When without asking or telling, for it was not the day of such, the feet drop away and the trail cannot be felt. The heap sits atop itself and the silhouette atop the distance. Beyond distance that lay under the feet, lay the exempt. How else to say?

37

Makar Sankranti

THE utensil vendor said that it is Makar Sankranti today. It is a major festival amongst us Hindus. The tailor informed me that today marks the day in the calendar from when days will begin to get longer and nights shorter; and that it signifies the beginning of the harvest season. Beyond this they did not know about Makar Sankranti, nor did I. Though no one knew which deity was to be worshipped on the occasion, the festival was celebrated with vigour and earnestness as in a family. The utensil vendor's wife—a woman of much warmth and motherliness—had prepared *laddus* (sweetened balls) of sesame and jaggery for the occasion. We ate some. It was followed by performing a few minor rituals and prayers for the well-being of one's self and family, and the ceremony lasted no more than ten minutes. Celebrations over, everyone returned to their daily life of hawking and selling as usual. I did not enquire more of the festival than I had seen or been told.

I met the tailor, betel-leaf seller and utensils vendor in Shahberi village during my walk a few evenings ago. We meet now and then. Usually, we chit-chat, talk of social or religious matters, about the ways of the new generation of youngsters, discuss anecdotes from mythology, talk of rising prices or the prevalent politics in the local traders' association. There is rarely anything more that we talk about; but we meet again and again. Our conversations are interspersed with much light-hearted gossip, too.

Upon returning home I recalled that in the region where I grew up, about the only ritual observed on Makar Sankranti used to be worshipping new crops and eating *khichdi* (rice and lentil cooked together) with *ghee* (clarified butter) or buttermilk. People applied mustard oil to the horns and hooves of livestock and put garlands of cowries around their necks. A few flew kites on the day. There is, indeed, much more that we did not know of; but Makar Sankranti is not the purpose of this writing.

Meeting the tailor, betel-leaf seller, utensil vendor or others like them keeps my educated self's hunger to know more restrained and grounded to some extent. Their indifference to knowing is heartening. To know and practise only little or nothing, or only so much as is commensurate with one's station, I find, is a sane way of living.

For long I have wondered what Hinduism (or any other religion) means for people like them in the countryside. Irrespective of religion, they form the huge majority of the population in India. Certainly, they are not a knowledgeable people and know very little of even other matters. Amongst the Hindus, most have perhaps not even *heard* of the several sacred texts and scriptures beyond the Ramayan, Mahabharat and possibly a Veda or two. Of those that most people have heard, they do not know more than the rudimentary; and may not have read even one in its entirety. Almost all they know comes from hearsay (euphemistically called oral tradition) over generations and from watching *Ramleelas* or *Krishnaleelas* (folk re-enactments of the lives of Lord Ram and Lord Krishna) organized in some parts of their native region. Yet, theirs is a far more conducive and educative companionship; far more enhancing and heartening. Why do they not feel the need to know more and accordingly live the profounder and richer lives propagated in the sacred texts and scriptures? Why does this vast majority of people keep itself distanced from these learnings? Or, why do they crack an occasional joke about gods, learning and the learned? Why do they remain such that they are either denied the respectability accorded to scholars and the learned, or thrown to the margins? What makes them what they are? Taking someone or something seriously—or allowing themselves to be taken thus—is not their way of living.

Till three or four decades ago, like the Hindus, the Muslims did not know much about the Quran or Sharia. Talking of his youth, an illiterate and nonagenarian Muslim of shaved moustache and fulsome beard in Karachi (whose interview I saw on social media) had said, 'We did not offer namaz because there was no mosque in the village; nor a temple for Hindus to worship their gods. Neither felt a need as such.' He was talking of pre-Partition India when he lived in what is now Haryana in modern India. Though he had heard of the Holy Book, being illiterate he had not read the Quran, and neither had his contemporary Hindus read the Gita. In many ways he reminded me of the Hindus and Muslims and their run-down temples and mosques in my childhood village of the late the 1950s and early

1960s. Instead of the revered scriptures these villagers lived by each other and their landscape. But that, again, is not the purpose of this writing.

Although we were Hindus and Muslims by faith we were not Hindus and Muslims in our religious ways. We were social communities. Over time, how we became overtly religious I am not aware. Having celebrated festivals around lands, seasons, greenery, trees, sowing and harvesting, animals and planets, when and why did Hindus move to the sky gods and festivals around them such as Mahashivratri, Janmashtami, Ganesh Chaturthi, Diwali, Holi and others? When and how was the importance of the landscape replaced by that of the scriptures? I remember that in my childhood village we had heard of only Diwali and Holi among the festivals that are popular today; whereas Diwali was not really celebrated, Holi somewhat was. But we had not heard of Holika, the progenitor of Holi and the sky gods had still not reached us. There were festivals, beliefs, rituals, sayings, stories, anecdotes and jokes around cows, monkeys, snakes, ponds, wells, rivers, plants, trees, *sadhus* (Hindu holy men) or *pirs* (Muslim holy men). The mud-cave shrine of a male buffalo near my childhood village attracted scores of devotees every day and hundreds during an annual festival. Instead of a priest presiding over it, there was only a caretaker (a volunteer), sometimes not even that. It was away from the narrow road of very few vehicles but many ox and donkey carts that piled thereon. Our elders did not know why the buffalo was revered (there were many versions) or how and when the shrine came up. But revered it was. Similarly, in Chhipiyana village near Shahberi, there was an idol and mausoleum of a dog by a pond. It was revered as a sacred site for curing dog bites and other animal-related illnesses. Now, in my village, instead of the buffalo god's mud-cave there is a solemn and large temple for formal worship, offerings, priests and rituals right on the main road for easy access for motorists. A year ago, during a stopover at the temple, I could not spot the earlier away-from-the-road mud-cave shrine. The new temple is filled to the brim by the major sky gods of scriptural Hinduism and overwhelmed with many prayers, rituals and superstitions. The old buffalo god has only a small and insignificant presence in that temple.

Indeed, in my childhood village, though the Muslim was a Muslim, he was also half-Hindu. In the village, we Hindus ourselves were not Hindu enough when measured by contemporary yardsticks. 'Hinduism' was certainly not the predominant presence in our little lives and social milieu. There was nothing that was entirely Hindu or entirely Muslim. All lived in the same landscape and followed the same lifestyle, ate the same food, wore the same clothes, and had the same habits, values and social roles. The sense of religiosity was about the same amongst both communities, and it was not taken seriously.

For all practical purposes, Bhullan baniya was a Hindu. I did not know he was a Jain. No one knew; not even he. Two or three decades later, Bhullan was declared a Jain by religious experts, sociologists and other scholars whom he had neither heard of nor seen. Bhullan could not know on his own (or through other villagers) during his lifetime that he was a Jain. As one with a reasonably greater exposure to the world, I myself, upon growing up, did not know that fact. It is rather recently that I was told by a learned scholar friend that Jains are not Hindus or that Hindus are not Jains; that they are separate religions and their traditions and holy texts are separate too. Within Hinduism itself there are many traditions so separate from each other that each could be labelled a religion in itself; so must it be true of other religions. In everyday living for us, for all practical purposes, 'Hindu' and 'Jain' were interchangeable terms; they were the same in our minds and in their behaviours. It was only a few years ago I discovered that names such as Mahaveer, Ajit, Abhay, etc., are Jain names. We have always used them as our own Hindu names. Jains too use Hindu names. Jainism as a separate religion was unheard of and Hinduism remained much understated and under-practised. Bhullan was very much integrated in the village's half-Hindu community—certainly more than the sole Brahmin, Indu. At some point in the last forty or fifty years our shared sameness was torn apart by the learned discourses of informed and knowledgeable people we have neither seen nor heard of. Since then we have not known who or where to turn to, or what to make of ourselves. People used to be the same till recently: half-Hindus while Hindus were not full Hindus.

So, the tailor, betel-leaf seller, utensil vendor and his wife in Shahberi celebrated Makar Sankranti with vigour and earnestness, with an almost tangible distance from the scriptures and the sacred knowledge contained therein—suggesting in some ways that the scriptures are not to be taken seriously. 'They are there; let them be', they seemed to indicate. For them, scriptural religions, denominations and their espousal are to be taken as lightly as our chit-chat, village gossip or politics of the local traders' association. Except calling them half-Hindus I do not know which religious denomination to put them under. Or if there is even a need to do so.

Awaiting a haircut at the good old barber's shop this forenoon, I noticed a pandit ji in one of the two chairs. Whenever needed, pandit ji performs ceremonies, prayers and rituals in different houses for a fee. In typical orthodox Hindu tradition, he had just got his three-year-old son tonsured and a little choti had been retained quite in the middle of his little head to mark his Hindu denomination. However, whereas the son had been tonsured, pandit ji, the religious practitioner, got himself a fancy haircut. To be fair to his priesthood, he too had retained his choti in place despite the fancy cut, albeit the choti was a braided and somewhat stylish one. Though the tradition of tonsuring his priestly head is binding on him as much as it is on the son, he preferred the fancy cut. Now he was getting his facial hair threaded. It amused me somewhat that one who is devoted to God should be having his face threaded too. At the edge of his dhoti was printed multiple times '*Om*' (a sacred sound and invocation). From their conversation, pandit ji and the barber (a Muslim) seemed old friends. A picture of the holy Ka'ba was tacked to the mirror that hung above both men. Just that morning the electronic media had reported on, and gone hysterical about, the beheading of a Hindu tailor by two Muslim youngsters in Udaipur (Rajasthan) as a retaliation against some bad observations made a few weeks ago against Prophet Muhammad by the Hindu spokesperson of a political party. The majority of the media was full of anger, venom and incitement. It is certain that pandit ji followed the news and the aftermath of the aforementioned events on his cell phone (now being appropriately utilized by the son to watch animated shows) and the barber must have seen the same news on his phone. The pandit ji and the Muslim orthodox barber continued in their raw and earthy conversations, the disturbing Udaipur incidents not having had an effect. With much conviviality both continued in the best traditions of being true to their land.

There is much to do with the land and its metaphysics in the lives of the tailor, betel-leaf seller, utensil vendor, pandit ji and the barber. There may not be metaphysics without land. The little son of tonsured head and choti looks on at those around him and imbibes the traditions, and their India goes on. There is only little or none of scriptural religion in the lives of the common folk. Their ways come, every moment, from experiencing land—the small patch where they have lived for generations as half-Hindus, half-Muslims and half-Jains, and to where they know they will eventually return. Meanwhile, they live as wisely as humans can.

38

Of Identity, Eluding and the Place

Abandon false ideas, that's all. There isn't any need for true ideas. There aren't any.
—Nisargdutt Maharaj

JOURNEYS through a region and its people can be sensed only in the bones. Like all journeys, my journey too began long ago, in a manner of speaking, in the bones. I cannot say how long ago. Rarely is a beginning marked by an event or a moment in time. Writing of it, however, is quite the same as maintaining accounts and bookkeeping. This one cannot be any different.

Initially, I could not eat Abujhmad's food—boiled or roasted goat, crab, fish, jungle fowl, rat, wild vegetables or the occasional half-crushed red ants. Many a time the roasted food smelled like burnt human skin. On other occasions animal hair or other fibre had to be removed by hand before eating. Save salt, tiny wild green chillies (which were extremely hot and pungent) and the occasional tamarind, there was no other flavour to add to food. In some of the deep interior villages even salt wasn't available. For my first few months in Abujhmad I kept going to Narayanpur to fetch my rations of rice, lentils, onions, potatoes, tea leaves, sugar, milk powder, oil and a few elementary spices like turmeric. For the entire duration of my stay there, I could not master the art of making fire with flint and raw jungle silk that needed a fine twist of the fingers. So, I added matchboxes to my provisions to light the hearth. Gradually, however, the ever-simmering trunk of a fallen tree in the middle of the village began serving as my source of fire. But the other provisions had to be replenished frequently.

Walking back carrying the provisions over seventy kilometres was an onerous task. After two or three months, I procured a bicycle from Narayanpur. It was helpful in my descents through the forested hilly terrain. But when it came to climbs, it turned into a burden. Also, while fording the rocky rivers and streams, taking care of the bicycle, rations and myself all together was difficult. Many a time, instead of wading through the water bodies, one had to hop from boulder to boulder while crossing them. Balancing the laden bicycle as well as my own body at such a time was tricky. Sometimes the rations fell into the stream and kilometres of hauling, huffing and puffing came to nought. The trails, almost throughout their length, were strewn with pebbles, jagged pieces of rock, ditches and porcupine quills that sometimes punctured the tyres of the bicycle, and the punctures could be fixed only in Narayanpur. In any case, much of the time the cycle had to be walked instead of being ridden. Eventually, I gave it away to Manzar bhai, my tailor friend, with whom I spent many hours gossiping over tea in his shack in Narayanpur.

Till the time I finally turned to Abujhmad's boiled and roasted fare, I ate the easier-to-cook khichdi with potatoes and onions added, and an accompaniment of the tiny chillies. The lid of an earthen pitcher served as my plate till I got used to eating and drinking out of leaf plates and leaf cups without spilling anything. There being no tradition of making pottery in Abujhmad, the lid of the earthen pitcher too had come from Narayanpur. Sometimes, I sorely missed a sweet treat. Besides honey—not found frequently—there was nothing sweet to savour there. Many times, I missed tea rather badly but the nearest cupful was seventy kilometres away.

My first few months had been spent in wandering from village to village. I did not want to settle down in one as that strange somebody who had suddenly dropped out of the skies. People have sensitivities and their consent is needed. Abujhmadias are shy. Upon seeing me approach they would run and hide in the surrounding forest. Language was also a barrier and I could not communicate much with people. Whatever little communication happened—such as asking for water or whether I could stay the night in the village ghotul—took place through hand gestures. There were many instances when I simply walked into a ghotul and lay down for the day or night. No one objected or questioned me. By and by, I picked up a smattering of the local dialect. It is relatively easier to pick up a language when there are no other options to converse in.

Though Abujhmad's huts had bamboo walls, ghotuls did not. Without the security of being enclosed by walls, it was at first unnerving for me in the dark with tigers, leopards or bears lurking nearby. There were other creatures too that were believed to inhabit the surroundings in the dark. It was at such times that gods and ancestors had to be invoked to provide protection for nothing else may have worked. After having spent a day or two in one place, I would walk to another village. In the process, I happened to revisit many villages. Revisits came as blessings in disguise as people and I had begun becoming familiar with each other. The instances of them running into the forest at my sight were declining and dogs were barking less. (Like the Abujhmadias, their dogs are also shy and never chase a human. They are neither pets nor hunting dogs nor guard dogs; just dogs, like humans are just humans.) However, in some villages people would still speak with me from a distance, ready to hurtle into the vegetation again. By and by, though, an acquaintance was surely developing and the villagers' shyness diminishing. After about six months, the people of Garpa suggested I set up residence in their village instead of 'walking round and round'. That is how came to be, by Providence, my residence in Abujhmad.

But settling down was not without its issues. Even though I was happy, I did not have the faintest idea of constructing the hut that was to house me. That left the seven families of Garpa perplexed and a little dismayed. I had to explain my inabilities. Since I had no training—and could never have—in using the axe, Juru, Suku and Dunga felled the logs and cut the bamboo stems needed to build the walls; they fetched the tall grass to roof the hut as well. Under the central pole of the hut was placed a stray piece of iron to keep evil away. It took a few days before the hut was ready for me to move into. A fence of bamboo poles was created around the hut, making it a kind of consecrated space of well-being. Till the hut was ready to be lived in, instead of the ghotul, I took shelter in an abandoned hut near Burunga's hut. The ghotul was for the youngsters to spend the nights in, and ought not have been trespassed into again and again. Burunga was the blacksmith who was uninformed of even the basics of smithy or ironwork (an account is given elsewhere), just as the rest of Abujhmad. He was nevertheless known as Burunga the blacksmith. Garpa not only offered a stranger place to reside but also provided a hut and well-being. What magnanimity that was from a people who knew nothing about the stranger or his purpose of being amidst them!

Just as it takes one a few weeks to settle down after moving to a new city, it took me some time to get comfortable in Abujhmad. Living there was not as easy throughout the duration of my five years there; only the unease diminished as time went by. In many ways, the region was too often unimaginably different from—and contrary to—what I was familiar with. The unfamiliar and invisible villages of three or four huts camouflaged by the dense vegetation; a human being merging indistinguishably with a bush; the limited vocabulary and words, and counting only up to five reflected the people's measures that served them for everyday living. How does one fit one's large self and measures into the smallest of them? Each situation, notion or function of body that I had lived by till then was either non-existent or different there. Above all, the notion of 'man the doer' or the contemporary 'go-getter'—upon which is pegged the entire existence of the outside world—was almost completely out of place in the deeper areas such as the village of Ehnar. There was very little of the world but abundance of that which is not the world.

People's names were more like phonetic sounds than names. Usually, they did not denote anything, nor had they a meaning. The names Masiya, Mahangu, Juru, Sulki, Chaitur, Suku, Burunga, Faigu, Jali, Bulki and Kutli, amongst others, were sounds without meaning or associations. Were one to describe them, they may well be considered exclamations of sorts (there was much exclamation, in any case, in people's speech). Also, though people were known by these names, they were not their actual names. The actual was known only to the parents. It was not known even to oneself for the entire duration of one's life. Masiya, Mahangu, Sulki, Chaitur, Suku, Burunga, Faigu, Pilsu, Jali, Bulki, Kutli and the rest were like disguises the villagers wore, only versions of the actual. They were deflections careening away from one that will never be revealed. Unrevealed and insubstantial is the disposition of the wild and its Abujhmad. When one reached the village ghotul one's disguise too changed. All let go of their village names and took to ghotul names. They were the other wraps to be under. So, when I addressed Pilsu in the ghotul, sometimes I did not know who he really was. Moments earlier, in the village, he was Chaitur. In his parents' minds he was someone else. At the crowing of the cock in the morning, Pilsu would leave the ghotul and re-enter the village as Chaitur; 'Pilsu' would thus be deflected away from. But never would he or anyone else know his real name. This was what it was like addressing someone with two different names at different times of the day or night and at different locations while being aware that the unknowable third name alone was the real one. Disguising oneself like this each morning and evening continued for about the twelve or thirteen years one spent as a member of the ghotul. Upon marriage, one's membership ceased; so did the ghotul disguise. Never again would he be disguised by it, nor could he assume it again. Then there was only one disguise to go by, that is, the one he has to assume in the village and world. But that would not be the real name given by his parents.

Abujhmad was about dissolving names, identities and distinctiveness; it was about keeping alive a certain elusiveness.

Of Identity, Eluding and the Place

That one became somebody else at a particular time of the day and was treated thus by others reminded me of the impersonators in my childhood village in north India. Impersonators lived in the village or came from those nearby. The villagers knew who the impersonator actually was—his name, the community he belonged to, his parentage, the address and location of his house and the cattle he owned. But he was looked upon and accepted as what he had disguised himself and appeared as that day; he could be a high government official, a landlord, a policeman, a dancer, Yudhishhtir from the Mahabharat, an astrologer, Raja Harishchandra, or a shopkeeper from town come to collect his dues. All were caricatured well by the impersonator, who came from the poorest community. He was extended due deference or disdain as dictated by his assumed rank or station of the day. On the one hand, the onlookers took him seriously, with all the due protocols, but on the other hand, he was also greeted with amusement. Despite the awe, fear or scorn (whichever was appropriate for the day's camouflage) people displayed, they secretly whispered and laughed because it was only a disguise of the temporarily absented actual. This play of impersonation happened several times during the year and particularly at fairs.

What could the deflecting or circumventing of names and personas, amongst other things, in Abujhmad be about? I cannot say. But having been in that milieu for some time, I felt quite palpably that there was much that the region concealed under its wraps and ways. Inherent therein, seemed to be the suggestion to have the smallest of 'real' engagements with life and the world. The smallness of engagements was also reflected in the small vocabulary and counting, rudimentary ways of cooking and eating, tiny hut amidst vast and un-surveyed expanses, near complete absence of clothing, absence of details in everyday living, short distances walked in a day, or the non-existent practices of health, hygiene, craft and other institutions and practices. Man was only so much a part of the landscape as the tree, hill, stream, fly or fowl. Abujhmad was free, of even conscience and contempt. Much goes away when the landscape is torn apart. Theirs is the experience of landscape. It cannot be substituted by writing, knowledge or the awareness of it.

Not just with names but with several other things and phenomenon, many times it seemed that the region itself was a deflection. At least it appeared to look upon itself thus and live in a similar manner. Like names, villages, ghotuls and impersonations, the world itself becomes a disguise. Silence, stillness, inertia, inactivity and the absence of imperatives that the world outside lives by seemed suggestive of something that is neither life nor world. Such remained throughout the days and nights, week after week, month after month and year after year in people's everyday ambiance and lives. In many ways, it resonated powerfully with the memories of my childhood village and—I say with some certainty—with the rest of India's languorous countryside that I happened to be in now and then.

How does an outsider realign with himself then? Or with the region? Or the larger world around it? With the extrinsic as the sole referent, how does one coincide with the intrinsic? Or how does one sidestep both? What measure can one have of oneself? Or are they even needed? It was a phase of catharsis too.

The wilds have the tendency to quietly seduce and engulf. The brown face of the hill, where shifting cultivation took place a year ago, is now covered in green all by its own effort. In another year or two, the vegetation will be dense; and then it will become impenetrable in the years following. The wild engulfs itself and those that live there. Slowly and imperceptibly it grows, one way or another, on humans too. Like the greening of the brown hill face, inertia began sweeping over me. Slowly,

Of Identity, Eluding and the Place

I began sitting with myself without doing or deed. Gradually, it was no longer possible or desirable to know what time of the day it was, or what day, month or year. Nor were such details needed. The forest had engulfed them and made such nitty-gritty superfluous.

This is the legacy from the unlearned and unhewed that I wish to preserve for the rest of my life.

Journeys also begin when arrives the point of no return; when there isn't a 'forward' either. All locomotion ceases and things are yet in motion ceaselessly.

39

On a Birthday

I was born yesterday; January 26 of 1954.
    A friend enquired how I am feeling on this seventieth birthday. She suggested I write my thoughts down. I do not really know what the feeling is or how to put them into words; or whether a month from now I would even agree with the pitch of what I am now writing. No feeling persists, nor a thought. Such is not their virtue. They are not one's own. Nor is the place they come to—one's self—one's own. Vagabond like, all come from somewhere and return similarly.

But there is something about each human that persists. It does not come from anywhere, nor does it go away. It is already there when one comes to life.

Living is usually strange. It is strange that I am living. I am not certain what else living feels like. It has been a long walk; sometimes it felt longer than I wanted or could afford.

Much that one may never know of oneself is indispensable to one's living, and sometimes even when dead, too. Without such, life may not be. Some of it has been good and sometimes life has been unbearably long-drawn. Some were years and years of immense internal exertions; others of feeling like being nowhere. However, in hindsight, I do not recall even one that failed itself or me. I do not know how but I have survived a reasonably long time, sometimes against odds, as many amongst us do. Many times, it was difficult inside and outside; many times, I could say, traumatic and thwarting. Many times, I reached the verge and badly wanted to go away.

Being shy and hesitant is one of the first memories of my childhood. The predominant feeling that held sway was one of perpetually being at sea; I felt within that my presence in life was of an 'ad hoc' nature and this feeling took up residence deep inside me. It was as if the feeling was something I needed to prepare for in the future. There was the withdrawn within; I was one who harboured, perhaps I could say, a feebleness when it came to peering or reaching out in life. I could not know how this feeling came; nor am I likely to ever know. But the wish to camouflage and hide remained overwhelming. In some inscrutable ways, being in Abujhmad's wilds or other places was one such way of hiding. Often people meet other people to hide themselves; to not be themselves. Not being oneself, that is, to deny one's svabhav, is the ridiculing of oneself. There is much hiding and disguising in intermingling and social milieus. Mother used to say to me, 'You do not like humans.' I do not know what an expert of the human mind or behaviour would say of me, but who can be more correct than a mother about her offspring! That instinct to hide from people lives on in me even today albeit now on a lower key. Being away from everyone and everything is a home where I always want to be.

The home, school, markets, games, time, people, addresses, commuting over distances, locus, neighbourhoods, architecture, travels—everything around me, the whole milieu, was evidence of plans, purpose and drive. As though there was hidden behind these a grand consequence. It was too structured and unnecessary for a child's naiveté and innocence. They constituted a grand design for living a life; but at the end of the day, it was for an average and ordinary life. Yet all such plans and purpose seemed improvised and far too exerting to make much sense to me; at times, I felt they were vain and in reality ad hoc. The planned and designed looked juvenile. Almost all of my life I have been without plan or purpose and have had an instinctive aversion to forethought. Nevertheless, I accept that there is an evident efficiency to such milieu and its paraphernalia. Around me life seemed to be fervently striving to be sited and situated; fastened to a locus and address that in effect was not one's own. As I grew up over time, that emptiness within began emerging more and more and the feebleness within grew too. Emptiness was not in empty rooms, nor in solitariness; nor in quietly reading a book; not even in silences amongst friends, of whom I had very few. I could sense the emptiness ever so faintly during the three or four kilometres of somewhat tired walk back from school along the slender road of yellowed and worn-out grass. Often cattle and pigs lounged there and just as often there were sparrows and crows sitting atop them. Emptiness was in the dogs and their ways and the abandoned spaces they ambled upon aimlessly and ceaselessly; or in the similarly growing tall vegetation near home where came the howling jackals and hares in the evenings; or in the waters with algae that lay doing nothing; or in the bumblebee that whirred motionlessly and noiselessly above stale waters. Those are the places where I wanted to be, still do.

Camouflaged under countless names—homes, schools, markets, games, times, people, addresses, commuting over distances, locus, neighbourhoods, travels—we have congested ourselves. Even the vacant spaces within us are congested with thoughts, aspirations, intents, accomplishments, plans and other such juvenile titbit. They mob the bearers as does a pack of hungry wolves, tearing things asunder. No other creature does this to itself. 'Which class do you study in? There is a football match this evening in Sadar grounds. Which is your favourite subject? Diwali is next month or Eid is in the following. Who is your favourite teacher? Essays on a horse or on "Honesty Is the Best Policy" or "Is Science a Boon or a Curse." Such and countless more are marauders that mob the mind. Laid out all around us was much to know, think and do about; too much to carry on a single pair of shoulders. In such a milieu, meeting other humans was like choking oneself. Others were efficient and driven. I secretly longed to stay away from them. Such secret living was my hiding. With several stop-overs it culminated in Abujhmad and, in some measure, continues to this day.

I do not know how it got into me. As one lives on, one may choose to alter attitude, behaviour and habits but not one's inner disposition, the svabhav. It comes on its own; is of some unknown origin; and may be derived from a past life. I do not know. With the marauding mobs and incongruent svabhav, those were my years of feeling small, inadequate and secret. It continued well past my teens and into adulthood. There was much in the air, the milieu and mob to prod me to be something else; to not be true to my svabhav. Eventually, in the course of my sufferings over the years I had to begin learning how to not quarrel with my svabhav.

Estrangement from svabhav is quintessential atheism and self-exile. Wanting to change oneself is the unholiest sin.

However.

The stories in *Chandamama* made my little heart soar so high as it has perhaps never soared again. Father brought one each month. The imaginations stirred by those stimuli were something different. Except *Durgeshnandini* and *Vikram aur Vetal*, I no longer remember the stories in the magazines from decades ago but I do remember the unforgettable sensations and imageries they created in me. They reinforced conditions that were without purpose, plan or substance. However, readings of congestions, of meaningfulness, entered life as I grew older. There came the existentialists, absurdists, nihilists, socialists or even the religious texts. All wrote of meaningfulness or meaninglessness. The matrix was the same and formed of the opposite ends of the same spectrum. There were few exceptions like Premchand and Tolstoy, who, this way or that, soared to heights and recreated the emptiness I sensed within and while travelling on the slender road of yellowed and worn-out grass. However, after some years, and for some other reasons, I could not sustain reading.

Also, how can I forget the elderly tuition master who coached me when I was studying in class III or IV! Father thought I should be proficient at math. He thought it was good for the brain; everyone thought so. So, the elderly man came to tutor me in the afternoons soon after I returned from school. I never did the homework he set the previous day for I could not bring myself to do it. Nor could I bring myself round to doing homework or classwork given in school. There were many times when I jumped out of the unbarred classroom window (most schools used to be single-storeyed buildings then) into the little forest outside. As the elderly math tutor entered our house, I would not speak a word but look down in shame and guilt.

He would not say a word either but teach me the next lesson for an hour while my mind wandered far away on the three or four kilometres of the slender road of yellowed and worn-out grass, its cattle, pigs, sparrows and dogs, or the vegetation where came the howling jackals and hares, or the waters of algae that lay doing nothing. However, once the hour was up, the elderly teacher would carry me on his frail bicycle, huffing and puffing with the effort at his age. He would thus carry me on his bicycle for the next three to four hours, taking me house to house where he tutored other children. There, instead of asking me to sit down and pay attention to the lessons, he left me alone to be with myself and elsewhere. He nurtured that something in me that was extremely private and intimate, an anonymity against all. Never did he tell others or me why he took me along every afternoon at his age on a rickety old bicycle along those sweltering roads in summers. But I knew; he knew too. As though he had taken it all upon himself. Not a word, admonishment or disapproval do I remember over the year that he tutored me. He was teaching me more than math; somewhere something was happening and math lessons were only a guise and camouflage for it. Later, when I began reading Premchand and Tolstoy, it was the elderly tutor who always came to mind as a character wholly fitting their noble works.

In the cantonment of vast empty spaces resided the army regiments and battalions. Camouflaged amidst trees and shrubs, they were not easy to spot: somewhat like the Abujhmadia and the wilds I came to inhabit two decades later; or perhaps like the little forest of shrubs and trees outside the classroom of unbarred school windows. There was a veil to this cantonment; as there was to most other cantonments and also to my own withdrawn within. In such a concealment plan, purpose and efficiency appeared to be oddities and juvenile preoccupations. Also, overall, contours of shapes and forms as distinctly separate from each other had not till then extravagantly invaded the times or minds. The world had still not become fully explicit, full of shapes and forms of length, breadth and weight. When the world is made too material, all concealments are laid bare. Sitting on the back of the elderly tutor's bicycle, I liked going through those spaces. They held suggestions of something that I still do not know of. All I can say is that they were impersonating something else, practising a withholding of some unknown. Despite my elderly tutor's pains to teach me, and mine to learn, I am still poor at his subject; but deep within is the revered memory of the elderly man with a little bent back and stooping shoulders. The bespectacled and creased face with sweat running down, and the fatigued bicycle, are still with me. In hindsight, he was someone who had not come to teach me math. Math was a veil, as is all else. Life is lived tangentially and probably never directly or explicitly. There is never a direct line in the forest between any two points, the points being inexplicit too. There is hardly anything of the 'explicit' or 'direct' about life either. Math was the impersonator of something else. So, when the impersonators came visiting my childhood village, they both intrigued and fascinated me. There is something primordial to impersonations—the 'is and is not.' They are like conversations that do not go anywhere. Footloose like the *Chandamama* tales, they are adrift on currents not their own. Here, there or everywhere, without locus or address.

Over the years, and now entering the seventy-first of my life, many a time have I experienced the feeling that I may be called a failure in most, if not all, areas of life. But mercifully, like thoughts, such feelings too come and go. Never are they one's own. Vagabond-like, all come from somewhere and return similarly. One believes them at one's own peril.

I am glad at the strangeness of living. I am glad too that it has been this way. More than this I ought not know or think of.

This is what I am remembering and feeling on this birthday.

Acknowledgements

Landscapes, communities, and the sense of the tentative they convey also inescapably involve the surreal. There is a similar surrealness to skies, waters, vegetation, animals, vast and vacant spaces, forbidding darks of nights, the distinct hum of silence and stillness. There are the living interactions between natural and societal processes, highly localized and land-based modes of living, governance, non-profit economies and the eventual way of life. This was difficult for me to write about.

Chandan bhai, Musahar the elder in Parraiya, the old couple near Chilpi Ghati, Sarup, Burunga, beggar on the train, the elder at Marwari Basa, and village of Dedhuki are amongst those several who lived wisely. Themselves disengaged, they were deeply engaging; as though coming from another locus of life. Without them these writings would not have been possible. Even though removed by hundreds of kilometres, their ways of 'self-neglect', discreet distance from worldly accomplishments, leaving much (if not all) room for inactivity, or keeping the details of everyday living unmeasured, uncertain and nebulous were the same. To them goes my utmost gratitude. In them resonate in some deep albeit dwindling ways the mystiques of lands, landscapes and wilderness. Indeed, I have been fortunate to have known them.

My thoughts go out to friends with whom I shared and discussed several aspects of my experiences, observations and ruminations. My gratitude goes to them for hearing with care and persistence, and the significant feedback they gave.

I am no less indebted to my mother. My conversations with her may not have happened with anyone else. Her memories since around 1920 of her village and times cannot be found in books, seminars and histories. Practically unread, she gave the much-needed breadth to my experiences and understandings. The arguments, as though, came from another sensitivity and concern. I am as thankful to my daughter Kunalika, who was the first person with whom I shared my experiences of the countryside—the people, wilds, animals, silences, vast vacant spaces, trees, the small villages of distant obscurities and the rest. It was her keen interest as a child that spurred me to begin writing in due course. Much is owed to this my first audience.

I am expressly indebted to HarperCollins India for their editorial help, time and expertise towards helping improve the quality of the manuscript. In my short journey as a writer, they have stood by me. Above all, I am thankful to them for bringing these writings out as my third book. Sans HarperCollins India it may not have come out. My special thanks go to everyone in the publishing team.

About the Author

Narendra's journey into the regions of wilderness commenced in 1980, when he began residing in the remote and pre-agricultural Abujhmad region of Bastar (Chhattisgarh) under a field-research programme of The United Nations University (Tokyo) and the Centre for the Study of Developing Societies (New Delhi). After spending five years in Abujhmad, he continued residing in adjacent areas of Bastar, focusing on conversations and expressions centred around wilderness, land, water and the natural-ecological cohesions inherent in the daily lives that sustain the mystical adivasi sensibility and way of life.

Throughout the years, some of Narendra's writings have found a platform with Dark Mountain (UK), Earth Island (USA), and Chelsea Green Publishing (USA). He is the author of *Bastar Dispatches: A Passage Through the Wilds* (HarperCollins, 2018) and *A Sense of Home—Abujhmad and a Childhood*

Village (HarperCollins, 2020). A book in Hindi was published by Prabhat Prakashan, Delhi, in 2022. Another one in Hindi is under publication. A rendering of his works into Marathi is nearly complete.

Narendra has also shared his insights on the intertwined themes of tribal and folk cultures and communities through talks at various national and international forums.

Presently, he resides in Noida, Uttar Pradesh.